Riley Edwards-Raudonat, Uwe Gräbe,
Kerstin Neumann (Editors)

Mission in Solidarity –
Life in Abundance for All

Beiträge zur Missionswissenschaft / Interkulturellen Theologie

herausgegeben von

Dieter Becker und Henning Wrogemann

Band 41

LIT

Mission in Solidarity –
Life in Abundance for All

Proceedings of the
EMS Mission Moves Symposium
in Bad Boll 2017

edited by

Riley Edwards-Raudonat, Uwe Gräbe,
Kerstin Neumann

LIT

Cover Image: B-Factor GmbH, Stuttgart

This book is printed on acid-free paper.

Bibliographic information published by the Deutsche Nationalbibliothek
The Deutsche Nationalbibliothek lists this publication in the Deutsche
Nationalbibliografie; detailed bibliographic data are available on the Internet at
http://dnb.d-nb.de.

ISBN 978-3-643-90952-7 (pb)
ISBN 978-3-643-95952-2 (PDF)

© LIT VERLAG GmbH & Co. KG Wien,
Zweigniederlassung Zürich 2018
Klosbachstr. 107
CH-8032 Zürich
Tel. +41 (0) 44-251 75 05
E-Mail: zuerich@lit-verlag.ch   http://www.lit-verlag.ch
Distribution:
In the UK: Global Book Marketing, e-mail: mo@centralbooks.com
In North America: International Specialized Book Services, e-mail: orders@isbs.com
In Germany: LIT Verlag Fresnostr. 2, D-48159 Münster
Tel. +49 (0) 2 51-620 32 22, Fax +49 (0) 2 51-922 60 99, e-mail: vertrieb@lit-verlag.de

e-books are available at www.litwebshop.de

Contents

PART 3: THAT THEY MAY HAVE LIFE, AND HAVE IT
ABUNDANTLY

*The Participants of the EMS "Mission Moves" Symposium, Bad Boll, June 2017.
Photo: Sambo/EMS*

Preface

Uwe Gräbe

It was a bold step when, back in 2012, the governing bodies of the *Evangelical Mission in Solidarity* (EMS, at that time still the "Association of Churches and Missions in South West Germany") started proceeding toward full internationalization. What used to be a dichotomy of German "member churches" and international "partner churches" became a *fellowship* – or rather a *community* – of churches and mission societies worldwide. All member churches of EMS – whether in Africa, Asia, Europe, or the Middle East – have been invited to share their spiritual and material resources, and to bring forward their ideas and contributions toward a common future.

Certainly: Other mission societies had taken similar steps prior to this. However, it is no exaggeration to say that the diversity within the EMS community is quite extraordinary. In this regard, let us not forget that as early as 1972, three very different mission societies (the Basel Mission – German Branch [BMDZ], the Evangelical Association for the Schneller Schools [EVS], and the German East Asia Mission [DOAM]) had brought their respective ecumenical and missionary networks into the then newly established EMS. Moreover, the German churches who joined them in this endeavor were not of one mold, but represented different Protestant traditions.

The ramifications of internationalizing these networks with their different spiritualities, theologies, cultures, and mentalities – all within one fellowship – are far-reaching. Suddenly, it becomes apparent that within such an international community, there is no "normative" approach to mission. Well-established perceptions of evangelization or missiological concepts in one church are challenged, unexpectedly, by the totally different approaches of another church. Projects and programs that seem theologically dubious in one part of the international community are held in high esteem by representatives of another part of the very same fellowship. Last but not least, this has repercussions on where to invest financial resources, and where not.

It might have been an option to commission experts, theologians and missiologists, to examine and explore these very dynamic processes of internationalization. The EMS, however, chose a different approach: In November 2013, the EMS Mission Council resolved that *"EMS members shall be invited to examine ('mirror') the understanding of mission of other EMS members and BMDZ partners. The various expressions and evaluations are then collected as a basis for a EMS symposium on 'mission moves'."* In 2014, the EMS General Meeting confirmed this resolution. At the same time, the General Meeting resolved on a multi-year "EMS Focus" , encouraging *"the churches and missions in the fellowship to actively participate in the programme"* titled: *"Life in Fullness for All – Mission in Solidarity"* (John 10:10). In other words: The task of examining that broad spectrum of mission approaches within the EMS has been entrusted to its own *grass roots*: to church members from three different continents, to women and men, clergy and lay, theologians and non-theologians alike.

The first steps in this process were taken in 2015-2016 with the four so-called *"team visits"* to EMS member churches in Ghana, India, Indonesia, and Germany. While the four teams were highly diverse with regard to age, gender, and nationality, they had in common the fact that *they were not made up of "experts" for the countries and churches visited, but rather of "strangers" to these respective contexts.* The observations and results drawn from these team visits were merged into detailed reports, which became the basis of a *"Mission Moves Symposium"* under the title *"Life in Abundance for All – Mission in Solidarity"* (the terms "Fullness" and "Abundance" being quite exchangeable) which took place in Stuttgart and at the Protestant Academy Bad Boll from June 5-9, 2017, and which was attended by a good number of team visit participants, stakeholders from EMS member churches, Mission Council and Secretariat, as well as a few external experts.

The Symposium was prepared by representatives of different EMS member churches and mission societies based in Germany, namely Heike Bosien (Evangelical-Lutheran Church in Württemberg), Rainer Lamotte (Protestant Church of the Palatinate), Diks Pasande (Protestant Indonesian Church in Luwu, and at the same time ecumenical co-worker at the Protestant Church in Baden), Riley Edwards-Raudonat

(EMS Secretariat), Uwe Gräbe (EMS Secretariat and EVS), and Kerstin Neumann (EMS Secretariat) – the latter three being also the editorial team of this book. This same preparatory group with the addition of Emmanuel Kwame Tettey from the Presbyterian Church of Ghana, also drafted the first outline of a Communiqué, which then was discussed, edited, amended, and resolved by all Symposium participants.

Those responsible for the Symposium were privileged to work in close cooperation with the Evangelical-Lutheran Church in Württemberg which, on Whit Monday, June 5th, 2017, and on the occasion of the 500th anniversary of the Lutheran Reformation, held its "Festival of the Worldwide Church and Mission" under the theme *"There Blows the Wind of Freedom" ("Da weht Freiheit")*. Hence, the closing lecture of the Festival was at the same time the opening lecture of the EMS Mission Symposium. This lecture dealt with the question of: *"Mission – Religion – Values… in a fragmented world: Mission as Connection"* (Rima Nasrallah van Saane).

In the first part of this book, we present the lectures given at the Symposium. These lectures were meant to assist the team visit participants in better understanding their experiences as "strangers" in a given context, to contextualize their impressions and to pinpoint them within a broader cultural, theological, historical, and missiological scope.

In part two, we have compiled some relevant excerpts from the reports of the four team visits. These reports were the basis of the hard work done during the Symposium. In working groups, the participants fine-tuned their findings according to themes relevant to the future theological profile of the EMS community. Finally, all this converged in the *Symposium Communiqué,* the focal point of this book's *third part*. However, since our humble endeavours would be in vain were they not rooted in God's Word, this third part also contains a reflection on "Reading the Bible through the Eyes of Another", a method used during the Symposium, and the sermon preached at the opening worship of the Mission Festival on Whit Monday.

The reflections presented in this book represent the conclusion of an inspiring activity conducted throughout the EMS fellowship. At the same time, they are a point of departure. From here, we continue to grow together in faith and witness as a global and diverse community of believers in Jesus Christ.

PART 1: CONTRIBUTIONS TO THE SYMPOSIUM

Opening Address

Jürgen Reichel

The Preamble of our EMS Constitution from 2012 succinctly defines the purpose of EMS as *"uniting churches and mission societies as equal partners in the common witness to the Gospel of Jesus Christ".*

All the elements of this short sentence are important for our conference:

- It starts with the *uniting* aspect of the fellowship of churches and mission societies. EMS ventures to bring together groups from many different backgrounds – geographically we come from Asia, the Middle East, Africa and Europe. Even within these regions we are quite different from each other. EMS is not a homogenous body when it comes to confessional or dogmatic questions – we stem from different Protestant and Evangelical traditions which could under other circumstances challenge each other or even make the discussion impossible. Ethical questions in our respective environments and contexts lead to different positions, and very often we have to admit that our Christian way of life reflects the general convictions in our home culture and differs from how Christians in other cultural contexts live their faith. But those who decided to form that family of churches and mission societies called Evangelical Mission in Solidarity put the sense of unity above everything that divides us. Let us be very aware of this at a time in which nations and religions are tempted to insist more on what separates them than on what unites them. Let us continue to build common spaces.

- The second aspect: we come from *churches and mission societies.* As we all know, the relation between the two has not always been simple. In the 19th century, mission was one of the first expressions of civil society in Europe. Missions were not created by the churches, but citizens and farmers, craftspeople and merchants joined the mission movement and founded mission societies. Mission was a movement that looked to the future and dared to cross frontiers. Pietism and enlightenment went hand-in-hand and found the spiritual and economic resources that led to the proclamation of the Gospel all over the world. EMS honours this element of pious freebooting and the spirit of enterprise which used to be a marker of the mission societies. As a mission today, we feel supported by churches and missions likewise to take up traditions and ways of doing things but also to seek new ways of communicating the Gospel.

- The third aspect: *equality* is one of the pre-eminent features in EMS. The fellowship consists of large churches with millions of members, and smaller ones with only a few thousand people. Some contribute generously to the manifold tasks of EMS; others restrict themselves to the membership fee. But within the life of our fellowship, especially when it comes to participation in programmes and in the decision-taking bodies, members have equal rights. In EMS, we are convinced that everybody has something to say and something to share. We appreciate the wisdom of the grassroots churches, the testimony of the marginalized and the voice of those who normally do not have a say. We encourage women and the younger generation to take part – as equals among equals, and we acknowledge lay people as much as those who lead their churches.

- And a fourth aspect: we seek to witness to the **Gospel of Jesus Christ together**. In EMS, we do not follow an idea or a vision, but put our trust in God′s own Son. For us, Jesus from Nazareth came to serve the poor, to teach the marginalized and to heal those who suffer. Jesus came to bear the cross and die as a criminal but rose by God′s grace into new life. He calls us now through his Spirit to proclaim the good news of God′s coming Kingdom. The Gospel of Jesus Christ is the one treasure that we Christians know.

The Heidelberg Catechism expresses it nicely in its first question: *"Question: What is your only comfort in life and in death? Answer: That I am not my own, but belong— body and soul, in life and in death— to my faithful Saviour, Jesus Christ. He has fully paid for all my sins with his precious blood, and has set me free from the tyranny of the devil. He also watches over me in such a way that not a hair can fall from my head without the will of my Father in heaven; in fact, all things must work together for my salvation. Because I belong to him, Christ, by his Holy Spirit, assures me of eternal life and makes me wholeheartedly willing and ready from now on to live for him.*"

So we come together as the Evangelical Mission in Solidarity - a community which "unites churches and mission societies as equal partners in the common witness to the Gospel of Jesus Christ". We have shared many things together: We have visited – as equals, men and women, younger and older people. We came from different regions and different backgrounds and explored how the Gospel of Jesus Christ found its way in the Donggala Church and the Church of South India, and in the Presbyterian Church of Ghana and in the Protestant Churches of Baden and the Palatinate.

You were the EMS messengers of that enterprise which was called into life by the Mission Council in November 2013 in Lambrecht. It was the second meeting of a Mission Council under the new constitution which determined the internationalisation of EMS. Representatives from Korea and Japan, Indonesia and India, the Middle East, Ghana and South Africa met with Germans who until 2012 saw EMS as their – somehow German – mission society. They now formed international bodies, and one of the first tasks they undertook was to create the "Mission Moves" Programme. The Mission Council decided at that time to work as an international community on theological questions: How is the Gospel of Jesus Christ understood in our different contexts? How do we witness to our faith? In how far do "changing landscapes" - as the World Council of Churches puts it in its Mission Declaration 2013 in Busan - change the witness to the Kingdom of God? And what exactly do churches and Mission societies in EMS describe as our joint mission?

As you can see, the Mission Council did not want to push that crucial question through. They thought it necessary to take time – time to experiment, time to get to know each other better, time to learn to appreciate differences or to find out that perspectives might not differ so much. They did not commission a working committee to propose texts and definitions, but asked you to become participants in a joint process – people of different ages, men and women, with different roles in their churches. They did not appoint a committee of theologians that could have worked on existing basic theological papers – like the above mentioned Busan Declaration on Mission. They wanted you to become familiar with at least one of the other member churches and to initiate the process of discussion and reflection during your visits in Indonesia, Ghana, India and Germany. The "Mission Moves" Symposium is a moment of convergence, where we begin to shape our common understanding of mission. The process as such is open because God´s history with God's creation and people is open, but as EMS we will set our milestones in the movement of the approaching Kingdom of God.

We thank the churches in Ghana, India, Indonesia and Germany who invited you to be their guests. They listened and asked questions, understood and commented. We thank your churches and mission societies who sent you as messengers and spokespersons and allowed us to learn from your experiences, your faith, and your vision for that EMS Fellowship. We thank all of you as you opened up in the team visits. And we are grateful that you are here now to allow us to profit from your experiences and your wisdom.

May God bless our beginning, our time together and all encounters and discussions. May it help to build EMS as a fellowship of "churches and mission societies as equal partners in the common witness to the Gospel of Jesus Christ".

Understanding Mission in the EMS Context:
Today's Challenges

Kerstin Neumann

Representatives of the team visits, members of the Mission Council, guests, colleagues, friends,

It is indeed a very special moment to welcome you all to the EMS Symposium "Mission Moves" that we are opening today. The room is filled with the joy of teamers meeting after quite a long time and sharing memories of intensive encounters and discussions. We are coming together now to pool our experiences of four team visits, taking them to a next level of reflection; as EMS general secretary Jürgen Reichel has just said: the symposium is a moment of coming together.

I have been through our team visit reports again. They are very rich and deep in the presentation of these experiences. We were mixed teams composed of different age groups and genders, representing EMS member churches with diverse traditions. The inviting churches received us in a spirit of friendship, this being the long-standing and cherished tradition of EMS members. In an atmosphere of open-mindedness they were well prepared and ready to give testimony. They gave us a chance to experience the life of the church, invited us for dinners, into schools and colleges and showed us selected projects of their diaconal engagement.

All the teams underwent the experience of being 'strangers', each member having to cope with the feeling of being 'out of context', having to forego the familiarity of otherwise unquestioned habits and forms of reflection. Not being able to understand fully easily leads to a sense of insecurity: this and the fear of losing control and balance were frequently expressed feelings during the regular sharing sessions. We were exposed to a variety of opinions that obviously made sense in contexts from where they derived but not necessarily in the context of the visited church. There were moments of awe and respect when we were confronted with challenges our host churches face and while gaining a sense for the commitment with which they go about their work.

There were times of discussion and argument during the encounters, and difference of opinion within the teams that we learned to understand as culturally conditioned, and that we could clarify and cherish while talking to one another.

Let me come to the two first conclusions:

- Our reports talk about the affirmation of diversity in EMS. Team visits confirm the extract that Jürgen Reichel chose and interpreted from the EMS constitution: we have travelled and acted as representatives of all our EMS partners and affirmed the deep sense of equality in our common witness to the Gospel.
- Personal relationships count! Doing things together, exchanging views face to face and experiencing together what it means to be stranger in an unknown place. Difficulties can be overcome, differences be brought to light when we relate personally and with authenticity.

This is a wonderful result of the visits for all who participated in the teams, as well as for the hosting churches.

How can we now translate this experience for the whole of the EMS family?

It is an important exercise to trace, outline and discuss common grounds of OUR MISSION, especially in view of the global challenges we face; the challenges, we found, differ according to the context and have to be addressed considering the differences in our respective circumstances.

- Religious expression can reflect wisdom, love and compassion; it can also be used ideologically as a support system for oppression and exclusion and therefore increase interreligious conflicts.
- The apparent gap between a form of Christian culture which is preoccupied with issues of personal morality, which affirms authoritative leadership, and which is committed to active, sometimes even aggressive, evangelism, emphasising the Holy Spirit as the all-decisive agent of faith, and – on the other hand – secularism with strong scepticism towards religion itself and its institutions, religion being just one option among many others to find meaning in life

What is our common understanding of mission in the EMS Fellowship in the face of contemporary challenges and trends?

Can our communion of churches and missions formulate a statement on mission we all could accept and support?

Mission is at times described as search for a new humanity, a new community. I like this approach. It reminds me of the overall EMS Focus motto for the years 2015-2019 which is taken from the Gospel according to John, chapter 10:10 asking for "Life in Fullness for All".

Mission intends to bring all of us into such a community of life, thereby overcoming geographical distances, cultural differences and theological outlooks. Mission brings together those at the centre of power and those at the margins. Such togetherness of ALL must be talked about, lived and dreamt. If it wants to be authentic, it must be worked out. Are we ready to argue, discuss and quarrel? We can do it because the basis of our togetherness is firm – it is the fellowship we share in EMS. We know each other and many of us share the same mission tradition. We have grown together and have made big decisions (e.g. the internationalisation) together. At this juncture, five years into the internationalisation, the Focus activity 'team visits' being completed, let us check where we stand right now.

For this purpose let us get down to very practical questions and to some of the challenges that we face and that need discussion. Here are two examples:

1. The Ecumenical Volunteers Programme is financially supported by the German Ministry of Economic Cooperation and Development: clear guidelines inform participants that they are free to express their faith or not. EMS accepts the religious and ideological neutrality of the participating volunteers as this is part of our affirmation of diversity in expressing and living ecumenism. Friends and partners in Africa, Asia and the Middle East find it difficult if youth volunteers choose to not regularly attend Sunday services. What is considered a most natural expression of faith in one country is considered a curtailing of freedom in the other.

2. During the last meeting of the international committee to decide on the financial support of projects and programmes of the EMS fellowship a discussion developed about whether we should cooperate in one particular project with an evangelical Christian organisation. Some felt that due to the confrontational form of evangelisation of this organisation, the cooperation should be rejected. Others argued that the organisation was doing good work and therefore cooperation should be appreciated. It became clear to the committee members that it needed to develop its own guidelines or recommendations for the common task of evangelisation.

    When we think of a joint understanding of Mission and Evangelisation in the EMS fellowship we should consider what WITNESS TO THE FAITH means to us. This must also be done in view of the fact that more and more member churches have to deal with at times dominant Muslim neighbourhoods.

    Could it be helpful here to differentiate the individual church's development from the joint programmes and activities as EMS Fellowship?

There are many other related topics found in our reports which we should have a closer look at:

- What is our position on interfaith dialogue which involves the question whether our Christian faith is to be understood as an absolute truth? Can we formulate a common position on our relationship to people of other faith traditions and secular ideologies?
- What is the role of diaconal work in mission? In what way is diaconia part of mission?
- This leads to another complex set of aspects around the question of HOW we do mission.

Mission takes its origin from God – *missio Dei*. All human beings are part of God's salvific action in history. We therefore consider ourselves as witnesses to God's mission in and with God's creation. What exactly it means to be witness needs further elaboration. Is it a humanisation and active participation in struggles for justice and liberation and/or a stronger focusing on conversion as a transformative change in a person's life?

Our discussions now during the Symposium, just like the overall discourse on mission, require a culture of hospitality and mutual respect. The diversity in the composition of this Symposium means that we need to respect the identity and freedom of the other while, at the same time, not forgetting to affirm and be faithful to our own identity. Authentic mission takes place when humans encounter God and receive the Fullness of Life that God offers.

I wish us all days of enriching discussion and the experience of being witnesses and part of God's mission.

Impressions from the Symposium – Photos: Waltz/EMS

Mission – Religion – Values… in a Fragmented World

Mission as Connection

Rima Nasrallah van Saane

Introduction

I recently remarked that in Beirut I feel as if we live in an airport terminal. Everyone around us seems to be on the move or hoping to move. Our weeks are marked by departures and arrivals. We bid farewell to an Armenian Syrian family on their way to Canada. We get in touch with an Assyrian Iraqi couple going to Australia. We regularly throw goodbye parties to young Lebanese emigrating to the US or the UK. We receive Ethiopian and Philippine ladies looking for domestic work and Egyptian and Bangladeshi men who end up in gas stations or on construction sites. Many of our students are constantly checking their phones waiting for a call from this or that embassy. The movements that we witness daily are part of global waves of migrations connecting all of us present here today as stations or nodes on this massive network of human mobility. Movement and migration are not new phenomena. However, the shape and scale of today's movements raise critical questions about the role and mission of the Church in our world. It has changed the way we perceive our own areas and the way we look at the others.

In this presentation, I hope to explore some of the issues surrounding contemporary migration and its impact on our perception of the other and the anxiety it is creating. Starting from our Christian understanding of who God is and how God works, I will try to propose concepts and metaphors that can inform our discussion of mission today.

Tangled injustice

When trying to explain some of the movements witnessed today, I find myself going further back in history and wider in geography. Why would an Armenian Syrian come to Lebanon on his way to Canada? And why should I call him Armenian-Syrian and not just Syrian! And how can I explain the plight of an Assyrian-Iraqi family in few sentences? In a world where simplified facts are preferred and black and white categories are the norm, rare are those who have the patience to explore the tangled reality of our combined sins. ISIS, Al Qaeda, or some Arab leader can be blamed; Iran, Hezbollah or even broadly Islam as a religion can be labelled as the cause of all ills. While not absolving any of these parties from the role they play in today's hot crisis, I would like to remind us that we are all implicated one way or another in the global and structural injustices that cause much of the movements we witness. Our colonial past still bears repercussions today. Deals made by world powers with opportunist local leaders drew artificial maps, displaced some communities and grouped others forcefully on the same land. Continuous foreign interference in the internal affairs of smaller countries polarises the already unstable communities.

Add to this the massive effects of our economic practices. From global economic systems to local consumer patterns, our unexamined lifestyles contribute a great deal to inequalities that fuel anger or feed despair. Those same irresponsible consumer patterns, in turn, bring about ecological pains that engender more human misery. To illustrate this complex matrix of injustice I will give the example of Northwest Iraq (Upper Mesopotamia) where great violence is witnessed lately and from which both refugees and extremists are exported. Past colonial and mandate powers have annexed this area to modern day Iraq while its inhabitants - a collection of varied ethnicities and religions - did not necessarily identify with that nation. These multiple ethnic groups such as Assyrians, Kurds, Turkman, Shabaks, Yezidis, Armenians and Mandaeans, some of which have a desire for independent states, inhabited it uneasily and regularly experienced or exercised violence and oppression. Foreign interference both from the West and from the East aggravated the situation by polarizing the different ethnic groups, arming them and then promising them untenable futures. Add to this the overlooked fact that for the past 20 years climate change has dramatically hit this area creating one of the world's worst water crises and almost annihilating the main economic means: agriculture, and thus creating more poverty and possibilities for local exploitation. And this is but one example where politics, economy and ecology intersect to create violence and propel people into movement.

Why am I mentioning this at a mission symposium? It is important as we keep exploring the concept and practice of Christian mission today that we start by bracing ourselves with both humility and attentiveness. In a world where post-truth has become an accepted dictionary entry and the masses are moved by made-up news, it is vital that as Christians we take time to explore the complexity of the situations at hand and not oversimplify matters. It is also vital that we approach them with humility recognizing that just as we can (and sometimes do) play a positive role in the lives of these moving individuals, we – as citizens of this world- are also implicated one way or another in the chains of injustice. Whatever we do in our earnestness to minister to the other remains wanting.

Moreover, this lack of knowledge and humility today is creating a general feeling of fear and is crippling the capacity of many to respond responsibly and sustainably to the changes at hand. We all seem to be gripped by fear and the concepts of safety and security are becoming our leading norms. We have come to love safety more than God and our neighbour. And if God cannot secure our safety, we relegate the role to our politicians.

Living in fear

One only needs to pass through an airport to realize again how terrified we are of each other. Security checks, alarms, cameras, secret agents, ways to trace people's records etc. An attitude of suspicion reigns in almost all the airports in the world. Every time someone wants to visit a country in the Middle East we are asked: is it safe? Embassies guide their citizens by providing them with coloured maps where safety is gauged by levels. And every time an attack happens, particularly in Europe, the fear barometer rises again.

We are afraid for our safety and the safety of our children and community. We are afraid that the other will kill us or harm us. We start eying everyone with suspicion and take precautions by taking distance from suspicious people or attempting to cut them off or isolating them. Yet it is not only our safety that makes us fear. We fear because as the flow of moving people increases in the world our local identities are at stake. We are threatened by that which is different and treat it as a danger to who we are because we *do not want* to change.

Moreover, we are threatened by unclear identities. Clear stable identities are easier to deal with. Yet, today rare are those who can identify themselves without a hyphen! A friend of mine is Chinese-Indonesian, one of my students is Tongan-New Zealander, another is India-British born in the UAE, as I was preparing this text my daughter who is Dutch-Lebanese went over to her friend who is Koran-Japanese-American, in this city we have Turkish-German, when we lived in the Netherlands our neighbours were Moroccan-Dutch. And the list goes on. Hybridity is threatening and makes us fear that we will lose grip on understanding society, clearly categorize it and identifying risk.

In his book *Following Jesus in a culture of fear*, Scott Bader-Saye explores our culture of fear in depth and reminds us that fear creates one of two reactions: retract or attack. While some big powers choose attacking when faced with fear, the rest of us retract. We retract by trying to draw sharper borders around our countries or our communities to protect ourselves and to protect our identities. It is no wonder that in today's political discourse the proposals for strict borders or even for separating walls are very appealing to those who are genuinely afraid for their safety, their future, or their identity.

Coming from Lebanon myself, I have experienced the culture of fear first hand. During the Lebanese civil war, Lebanon was divided in many different segments and Beirut itself was cut in half with a long impenetrable belt around it. Changes in the delicate balance of the various and competing religious and ethnic groups led to fragmentation. Each area was trying to host homogenous people who belong to the same religion or even the same denomination or political group. Separating ourselves we developed discourses about each other that vilified the other. Even after the war ended, the other remained suspicious and learning how to live together is still, until today, a daily challenge.

Today as more and more of us are mixing around the world, we see communities retracting and trying to build sharper borders around themselves and we are told that stopping the flow of people is possible and creating safe environment can be achieved by tightening border security. But is this really possible or does that also belong to the category of post-truth?

From fear to vulnerability

The experience of Pentecost is traditionally considered to be the launching of the missionary movement of the Church. Interestingly for our discussion, Pentecost is also the embodiment of the *reversal of fear*. After the resurrection and ascension, the disciples were retreating and recoiling from fear. They erected borders around themselves and closed the doors. They were afraid for their life and they remained an inward-looking group protecting their tradition. The day of Pentecost made them open the doors and go outside. From that day on, empowered by the Holy Spirit, they could connect to numerous people from foreign lands, from various ethnicities and cultures. Fear was brushed aside and they stood in all vulnerability and accepted to be ridiculed!

We stand in a similar context today. At our doorsteps, we have a multitude of nationalities, ethnicities and religious groups. I have read that here in Stuttgart more than half of the population are foreigners; in London more than 250 different languages are spoken, in Lebanon in a population of some 6 million we have 2 million Syrian refugees and half a million Palestinians, not counting all the other smaller groups with their different religious backgrounds. AND, we are all afraid. We are afraid for the present: what if among all these strangers lurk some terrorists! We are afraid for the future, what if the two million - mostly Muslim Syrians - will never leave and change the balance of religions again and alter the nature of our lifestyle? What if they take our jobs and ruin our economy? What if we get to a point where we are no longer able to control our environment? The values that seem to dictate our decisions these days are: security, prosperity and being-in-control (or as Britain called it: sovereignty). Therefore, it is no wonder that many are tempted to close their doors and only pass food parcels and relief aid from 'the windows'.

So what challenges does this present to mission?

Many of our churches have given up the concept of *mission by expansion* as we have known it in past centuries, mainly because despite leading to the spread of the church – it has also caused damage to both people and the Gospel. To go into 'heathen' lands or conquer new territories for Christ has proven to be ethically disputable. Yet, we are all convinced that we are called to mission. We look for new metaphors and images to guide us as we live this call, refusing to be 'colonial' and refusing to be a mere NGO that focuses only on development and relief. So, what images can help us perceive our role in God's world today; in a world where security, prosperity and sovereignty are values?

From expansion to connection

Many sociologists today describe our current realities with the image of Network. Manuel Castell's seminal work *The rise of the network society,* has triggered a lot of appropriation from the side of theologians who saw in the concept of network parallels with what Christians aspire and can learn from. Heidi Campbell, Stephan Garner, Dwight Friesen, Paul Hiebert and many others have been captured by this image and have seen in it a supporting structure for a contemporary theology and missiology.

The world of the internet has changed much in how we - as inhabitants of this planet - relate to each other. Thanks to digital networks we have come to be in touch with all sorts of people. It has facilitated the exchange of news, images and sounds and promoted the circulation of ideas transcending the limitations of time and space. It has helped us be present for each other and with each other across distances and instantaneously. It has made us realize how small our planet is and how closely interrelated we are.

In my opinion, what we experience in the concept of network as derived from the digital world can help us re-envision the way we go about mission in a moving and complex world.

There is a wonderful theological embedding for the image of network. At its core, the idea of network is rooted in our Christian Trinitarian understanding of God. The Christian God is 'a network' of relations, dynamic and egalitarian. Father, Son and Holy Spirit are connected to each other and relate in a dynamic flow of love. Not only is God, whom we have come to know in Christ, relational in the divine self - God also seeks relationship and invites us to connect and live in community with God and with others. The idea of a network is thus no stranger to the Christian faith nor to the way the Apostles were going about doing mission connecting towns, peoples and ideas to each other. Connecting Antioch, Thessaloniki, Derbe to Jerusalem and the Jews to the Gentiles.

Imagining mission as connecting through a network paradigm, slightly changes some of our strategies and expectations.

Instead of thinking of mission as sending and receiving, or developing programmes and implementing them, it shifts the focus to establishing networks and inviting people to connect; in Facebook language 'to become friends'. There is a very flat, egalitarian aspect to networks where hierarchy has no place. There is also equal opportunity, everyone can connect to a network whether rich or poor, near or far, man or woman, or whatever their skin colour is. Everyone can contribute to the network and enrich it with information and experiences. Networks are flexible and can be the *locus* of much creativity and dynamism. If we look at our social network online we realize how all the time that something is happening and new ideas are developing by people and from sides we did not expect.

Using the image of network helps us accept that people are not 'either in or out', 'either one of us or against us', but have the possibility to connect at their own pace, wish or intensity and from whichever side they wish. Even more, with each connection we make, entire networks are added to ours. For example, one of my husband's students is a Shiite from the South of the country. Good relations with this young man opened new networks which would otherwise be impossible to us and to the people we know. Our image of conversion as crossing boundaries, or a U-turn can be replaced by an image of people connecting relationally and orienting themselves to God and beginning a journey that hopefully leads towards Christ. Dwight Friesen, in *Thy Kingdom Connected*, says that in "the idea of networked Kingdom, Christians are formed and made more Christ-like as they continually encounter the living God, not just as a distant, future objective but also in and through the relationships with others – mediated by the Holy Spirit – in which Christ is present" (Campbell and Garner, 2016, 13).

I am fascinated by the image of network because it frees us from borders and separation and acknowledges our interconnectedness. It reminds us that we are connected to what is happening in Iraq, Korea or India through one or the other of our connections. It abolishes the artificial construct of East and West, North and South, us and them, donors and recipients and thinkers and executers.

However, connections are not neutral but have a quality.

The network metaphor encourages us to *value relationships.* To actively seek to establish relationships with others, between the others and with God. In order to connect and establish relationships we have to put down our guard and be open to others and wish to establish connections without fear for our security. Some would call that hospitality. Yet I am a bit careful with the word hospitality as it can sometimes insinuate that hospitality is about letting people use your space, enter your country, or be present in your town. However, connecting goes a step beyond to make sure a durable and just connection is established, and right relations that do not treat the other as object but as subject are secured. In a network, these relationships are not only bilateral (between two people) but are a grid that enlarges our world and the world of others and eventually lead to the God who seeks connection with us. The following quote from Daniel Migliore puts it clearly: "To be Christian is to participate by faith, love and hope in the new humanity present in Jesus, and that new humanity is one of renewed and realigned relationships" (Campbell and Garner, 2016, 82).

The network metaphor also challenges us *to be humble.* In a context of a network where everyone is equal, mission moves away from previous images of heroism where one party perceives itself as rescuing another. Standing on equal ground, we acknowledge that all goodness comes from God alone. It is not our human effort that is saving people but God's initiative. We are humbled as we realize that we do not own all knowledge nor can we control all factors. As Christians, our task is to ensure quality Christ-like connections with others and understand that connections have more than one node and the flow can be either way. We are open to receiving as much as to giving, to voice our opinion and to be challenged and be changed by the opinion of others. We are challenged to walk humbly with our God and be reminded that we are not gods.

Consequently, a network metaphor places us *in a vulnerable position*. While everyone around us is discussing how to be strong again and how being strong includes eliminating the threats and focusing on our own wellbeing, a Christian position is always a reversal of strength. By seeking connections with others and entering in relationships with those who are different from us, we can no longer hide from threats nor protect our identities. We have learned from Jesus that radical love of God and of others and an obsession with safety and control are contradictory. Jesus embodied for us the way God works in the world through human vulnerability. It is through his cross that we learn what love for God and for others means. It is not the strong, not the smart, not the powerful and rich who can achieve right relationships but those who accept to be vulnerable in the face of and alongside the others. Vulnerability is a challenge for the Christians of the Middle East who would rather fortify their position and defend themselves. Yet without opening up in vulnerability, no Christ-like relationships can be made.

And finally, the network metaphor challenges us to activate the command *"love your neighbour"*. Campbell and Garner in their treatment of networked theology ask us "who is my neighbour" in a network structure? Everyone is our neighbour today! Connected to each other means we share profoundly in each other's lives wherever we are. We have today the possibilities to learn about each other more deeply than ever. We are introduced to ethnicities and religions we did not know before. Today everyone is talking about the Yazidis while six years ago no one knew they existed. We can see, hear and participate in the lives of others in various ways. And we are constantly reminded how our actions, our words and our positions impact the others. The same Jesus who showed us love at work through vulnerability, showed that this love challenges unjust systems, political structures, economic practices and behaviours. In his boldness to counter and expose all the evil structures of his time he disregarded his own safety. Doing mission through our network connections means that instead of valuing safety, prosperity and control- just like the disciples at the day of Pentecost – we accept vulnerability for the sake of right relationships with others and with God. Doing mission with a network metaphor invites us to expose the networks of injustice and replace them with networks of just peace and life.

Mission – Religion – values… in a fragmented world

Travelling people need good connections. In a world where migration and movements of people are accelerated and threatening our communities, we need to establish better connections, better relationships, with each other and with God. When I was invited to do this lecture, I was asked the question: what would prevent a country from exploding when so many religions, clashing values and fragmentation arise?

We cannot prevent explosions.

Our experiences in the Middle East have taught us that war and violent clashes will keep erupting as long as there are different people in the world. However, we have also experienced the work and presence of God though good and right relationships despite the general atmosphere of violence and fragmentation. When people dared to be Christ for each other and see Christ in each other!

In the institution where I work, the Near East School of Theology, I found that one of the chief tasks we have is establishing relationships. Establishing relationships between the people from different nationalities in our area: Syrian, Lebanese, Armenian, Palestinian, Iranian and those who come to visit us from abroad: USA, Germany, Netherlands, Australia and others. Establishing relationships with the various eastern and oriental churches and church leaders: The Assyrians, Syriacs, Greek Orthodox and Maronites who have come to know us personally and are always glad to tell their story and present themselves to our visitors. Establishing relationships with Muslim leaders and their students, Sunnite and Shiites, conservative or liberal, who are invited to explain their faith and discuss it with us. By continuously visiting the others, barriers are broken. The other becomes a friend and then a friend of our other friends. The other is no longer an issue, a problem or a question: The problem of refugees; the issue of the Iraqis …. But a person …with a family, with health concerns, with hopes and memories. A person.

And this is how an Assyrian Iraqi couple, via our Assyrian Lebanese friends, can connect to us and we can connect them to our friends in Australia. This is how their story with all their complexity can be shared by others and how their life can be restored and new relationships established.

By getting out of the safe zones, we forgo the obsession with safety and we risk vulnerability. We experience the free flow of the Holy Spirit who acts creatively and who surprises us beyond our imagination.

The airport terminal we inhabit can thus become a hub, a network, where diversity and movement stop being threatening and become the environment to facilitating Christian love through relationships.

References

Scott Bader-Saye, *Following Jesus in a Culture of Fear, Christian Practice of Everyday Life*, Brazos Press, Grand Rapids, Michigan, 2007.

Heidi A. Campbell and Stephen Garner, *Networked Theology: Negotiating Faith in a Digital Culture*, Baker Academy, Grand Rapids, Michigan, 2017.

Manuel Castells, *The Rise of the Network Culture: The Information Age*, Willey-Blackwell, West Sussex, UK, 2010.

Dwight Friesen, *Thy Kingdom Connected: What the Church can learn from Facebook, the internet and other Networks*, Baker Books, Grand Rapids, Michigan, 2009.

Lively discussions at the Symposium – Photo: Waltz/EMS

Theo Sundermeier – Photo: Waltz/EMS

Aspects of Inter-Religious Hermeneutics

Theo Sundermeier

I. What does 'being a stranger' mean?

In Germany, where her father was on furlough, the little daughter of a missionary, who had been raised in Western Africa, saw some Africans at a railway station. She caught her father's hand and cried out: "Look, father, there are some real people!"

This scene focuses our attention on the question of what is familiar and what is strange. From an early age the girl had been familiar with African people, with their appearance, their ways of interacting with each other. Africans represented the familiar world of her childhood. They reminded her of her home. With the words "real people" she connected familiarity and a sense of belonging. It is not surprising that she did not name a distinction between the Africans and her parents, who looked quite different. Her parents *and* the African people together represent what she wanted to express. She felt at home again!

We should not over-interpret this example. Yet it reveals some issues which are relevant for our question. The moment of feeling familiar also contains the opposite feeling, the feeling of being strange. Strange yet familiar - only when related to each other do these terms convey the real question. They do not describe objective facts. They mark limits. Everything deviating from familiar situations is strange to us, while familiar situations are marked by what seems customary and close.

In Middle High German the term stranger *(vremde)* means a person who comes from a distance. Strange is what does not belong to the well-known place of residence but comes from the outside. However, not everything far from home has to be strange. In his famous definition, G. Simmel[1] says: The strangers on the star Sirius do not matter to me. They are not strange to me since they are unknown to me. What is strange to me is the *close* stranger, the neighbour coming from a distance.

---

[1] Simmel, 509.

"Strange" is a relational term. It is defined by the relation to the opposite. A subjective element is inherent to it. We cannot define something strange without this subjectivity.

We can distinguish five levels in which strangeness manifests itself as opposite to familiarity.

1.   The girl mentioned above spontaneously connected familiarity with the skin colour and physiognomy of the Africans she saw. That is the way she reacted to the most elementary experience of strangeness or familiarity. Similarity or identity define the familiar. Another skin colour signals difference. This has nothing to do with racism, but with the fact that originally our societies have been structured homogeneously. Where homogeneity is dissolved and makes way for a more complex structure, fears arise because an experience of strangeness is connected with appearance. It is the *appearance* which is remembered and makes one aware of strangeness.

2.   The experience of strangeness is intensified by the sense of smell. Smells separate even more sharply than appearance does. If in horror films smells of decomposition could be brought on the screen, this kind of film would quickly disappear from TV and movie theatres. I can close my eyes, I can look away, and I can get used to the sight of the stranger. The sense of smell, however, increases the difference. It is the organ of internalization. That may have its reason in the fact, that the olfactory nerves are directly connected to the central nervous system and identify strange smells as a danger. However, this is also due to the fact that the body smell is the most direct feature of a person and distinguishes him or her from every other person. Babies detect their mothers' smell as their very first impression even if they still cannot see. Through smell they learn to distinguish what is good and what does not belong to them. Smells are remembered and stick in one's mind even if the smell has passed. They evoke memories, they make limits disappear but just as clearly they also set limits.

3.   At the emotional level, sounds also cause feelings of strangeness, while at the phenomenal level they have a link-forging function. Sounds include both melodious sounds and dissonances.

Dissonances can be dissolved and changed into 'consonances' so that uneasiness turns into good-feeling. While strange smells cause defensive reactions, strange sounds force people to listen more sharply. Only if the dissonance does not end will a feeling of defensiveness emerge secondarily but getting used to the sound is also a possible consequence.

4.   Sounds connected to foreign languages cause a lack of understanding and displeasure but they do not cause enmity or disgust like the sense of smell. Sounds will more likely arouse somebody's curiosity to understand the foreign language. If this step is not successful, curiosity changes into indifference, an attitude which at any time can lead to curiosity, thirst for knowledge, and then to a turning to the other again.

Here another element of strangeness is recognisable. A *foreign language* is objectively strange to me if I have not studied it. Language promotes communication, it wants to be understood. We must try to learn the foreign language if we want to communicate with the stranger, or put ourselves on a third, common linguistic level of communication, the sign level. Understanding, however broken it may be, can be managed by looks and gestures. This presupposes a common basis of signs that make communication possible. This common ground is supported by the conviction that social life everywhere shows the same, or at least similar, structures. We submit ourselves to this common ground because we want to understand each other and communicate. This basic position is also necessary in our circle of acquaintances and within the family: we can only live together with other people and communicate if the given community is not constantly checked or put in question. But can common grounds really be presupposed in meeting with strangers?

5.   With that we have reached a fifth level of determining the feeling of strangeness and familiarity, the *social order*. It is characteristic of the order into which people are born and feel at home that they are not forced again and again to put it to the test.

Particularly people from western civilisations usually do not realise the limited validity of their implicit social knowledge. This is true especially in an age in which we are used to thinking globally and to ascribing universal validity to our world of experience, particularly when the capitalist economy and the natural sciences have gained world-wide acceptance and determine the world up to the most remote settlements. How much more deeply do we experience the shock, if the norm can no longer be taken for granted and is no longer valid in the private sphere, with our neighbour or with a school friend from another country. If in this way the validity of the self-understood is undermined and what till now has been considered to be 'normal' and correct, beautiful, pleasant and good is restricted in its importance or even called in question, then more than aesthetic and ethical rules of knowledge are at stake. Then culture as a whole, also one's personal and social identity, seems to be threatened. This feeling frightens people and causes hostile reactions.

It is not necessary to delve into the close net of social relations and mention all areas in which experience of strangeness can threaten human self-esteem. Instead, I will pick out those areas located in the centre of culture and which are occasionally considered as its bond: religion and the arts. In fact, I will focus on religion, and mention the arts only in passing.

In the encounter of religions these problems that come to light in the encounter of cultures are reflected in a concentrated form, perhaps still more biting, painful and aggressive, because religion touches the heart of human beings.

Although the linguistic derivation of the term *religio* is disputed, in fact the term absolutely confirms the point: religion means "bond", it binds the heart of people, it forms their life, determines their ethic and influences their aesthetics. 'Bond' does not only mean the bond with God but traditionally with the society, too, and the society also influences retrospectively religion itself. The increasing trend to make religion an individual and subjective matter is a phenomenon of modem times and in some respects is part of the nature of the Christian faith itself. From tribal religions — e.g. Shintoism was once one of these — which still are something like the 'basic religiosity' of all religions, we can learn how closely religion and society have originally been connected and have influenced each other. Religions determine people's way of life and rule out other structures of life. Religions bind people inwardly and set limits toward the outside and against other people. This means they offer people a home, give them instruction, offer counselling and in times of crisis catch them in a net of spiritual and ritual help so that they can overcome the crises in a community. But they banish those who leave the religious and social basic agreement.

The world religions link the believer to a declared creed to which truth is attributed and which expresses the truth. Thus they cognitively strengthen this basic binding structure of religion. By this confession to one truth other truths are virtually demoted to untruth.

The difference between what is familiar and what is strange is deepened and cemented by the encounter of religions. Because participation in worship services is not permitted to a person of the other faith, the lifestyle of the other person, their ethical behaviour or ideological convictions remain strange and inapproachable in the end. The partition walls are thick. Religion, which is supposed to connect, causes separation. Its signs and symbols, which strengthen internal cohesion, are at the same time a means of exclusion. The cross on a house excludes Muslims because they are not members of the church. Conversely, Christians know that the call of the muezzin is not directed to them, but to Muslims. On different university campuses in Africa thick trees had to be planted between the church and the mosque because "the half-moon is offended by the sight of the cross". The religious symbols become symbols of separation. They create their own worlds, their own space, their own field of relations which gives confidence to the members but signals to the other ones that they are not part of it.

In the cultural or aesthetic field, art has a similar effect to religion. It is to such a great extent part of the whole culture and determined by the respective religion and society that art also marks the difference from other cultures and at the same time concisely expresses the inner-religious awareness of life. However, the bounds of art are more permeable than those of religion.

Tribal tattoos, for example, the basis of all abstract ornamentation and wood carving of Africa, make tribal membership visible and their various meanings are only understandable to the initiated. This applies similarly to masks.

To mention a further example, Chinese art precisely reflects the conception of the world view of the Chinese people, which is characterised by Confucianism, Buddhism and Taoism. It has preserved its nature through the centuries as has the corresponding religious prevailing mood. Only radical socialism has superseded previous aesthetics and introduced a uniform socialist style.

It is a result of secularisation and the separation of culture from religion that our own art tradition shows such rich possibilities of variation; however, this is also legitimate and embedded in the idea of incarnation. The Christian message wants to have influence on a given culture and become 'incarnate' there, so that the message is formed by the influence of the surrounding world.

Islam has another vision. The prohibition of images or iconoclasm means that calligraphy has become the central stylistic means of expression of Islam but other artistic modes of expression, apart from architecture, could not develop, such as dramatic art, painting, and tragedy in the art of poetry. If Muslims are active in these areas, they must expect a charge of heresy which can lead to legal indictments.

In the following we will investigate whether religion can serve as a mean of connecting elements, changing strange things into familiar ones. First, however, we must ask how our culture has met the stranger until now. We summarize the ways of encountering the other in three different models.

II. Encountering the stranger

We distinguish three basic ways of encountering the other.

1.   *The alterity model*. The stranger is the enemy. The residential area or the country in which the tribe lives is home or a protection zone that grants safety. Outside your own territory is enemy territory. Whoever meets a stranger must regard him/her as a potential enemy. Here, in the unsettled area the Latin saying applies: *"homo homini lupus"*, "man is wolf to man". The pre-Islamic Arabs followed the legal maxim: It is not an act of murder to kill somebody in the desert. Since outside the home territory, an enemy was always also a potential

slave, the Ashanti called all people living north of them (the sea is in the south) 'slaves'. From Hegel, who defines the meeting with another as a fight between master and slave, we learn how deeply this fundamental attitude has been preserved in our culture till today. Victory or defeat, to subjugate or to suffer subjugation and lose national and state identity, this attitude that 'if you are not for us you are against us' *(Freund-Feind-Denken)* determined to a high degree the relationship between the European states until the 19th century.

2.   *The trader model.* At all times and in all societies traders have been exempted from this fundamental enmity towards the stranger. Traders are considered to be an addition, a resource as it were. We need traders. We need them as foreigners because they offer those goods that are not produced in our country and must be imported. Foreign traders are accepted, but only partially integrated. Definite residential areas are assigned to them. They have restricted rights only. In tribal societies and in the Middle Ages they could not marry a native woman. This ban was intended to prevent that some native families received preferential treatment because of loyalty to a trader's family. Ex-territoriality guaranteed the reliability of trade. For exactly this reason kings, princes, and even judges employed bodyguards, who had to be, and remain, foreigners. This was the reason for the pope to establish the Swiss Guard. Since they do not have any relationships to the native population, these foreigners are loyal to the prince. He guarantees them protection. The consequent ghetto situation is accepted by both parties. In times of unrest and danger, however, foreigners are easily branded as scapegoats and the ill-humour of the population is directed towards them, which shows the latent danger in which they live.

In Germany this kind of functional or partial integration exists to this very day. Nobody is bothered about a Japanese 'colony' in Düsseldorf as long as the Japanese observe their special status and do not give up their ties with Japan. Turks are welcome as 'migrant workers' as long as they keep their orientation to Turkey and return there. As 'guests' they are welcome but the permanent right of residence that has other rights as a consequence, meets with disapproval. Foreign traders who want to become local citizens will lose the goodwill they enjoyed before. They turn into a competitor and loses their special status. What made them attractive before - trading in strange goods and their own strangeness – is now felt as a threat.

3.   *The equality model*. A third kind of encountering the stranger negates the differences. It is founded on the conviction that all people are equal, think equally, trade equally, and finally have or should have the same ethical and moral ideas.

This idea is also held in psychology. Strange people as such do not exist; they are always the repressed self. Xenophobia is regarded as repressed or projected self-hate. This attitude suggests a boundless tolerance. Since, however, it is based on the presumption that strange people do not present any real alterity or otherness, but only reflect one's own being, tolerance comes up against limiting factors as soon as this basic assumption is called into question, and the stranger proves to be essentially different.

Are the differences levelled out in this model of the meeting with the stranger? Mostly they are, but frequently mixtures arise as you can see in the New Age philosophy of life. In the field of religion an artificial, synthetic syncretism is recognisable, the contours and inner logic of which are seldom reasonable. Arbitrariness prevails. The other religions serve people's own design and, depending on circumstances, are used like a self-service store, or a storage room if they are weary of a certain ritual or think it no longer necessary because it has done its job.

III. Hermeneutical levels

What methodical consequences for an inter-religious hermeneutic do we draw from our considerations?

1.   Understanding always requires that I really become aware of the other religion as another or different religion and respect its otherness. There is no place here for all the psychological efforts - recently *en vogue* – that regard the other as now being repressed. On the first level of approach towards the other religion and culture, we must perceive and observe its alterity. The first step requires distance. It is a matter of appropriate perception and description of the

phenomena. As in art-historical interpretation, great importance is attached to first grasping the phenomenological level as objectively as possible, i.e. without judgment or prejudice. At first we must refrain from any verdict.

2.   At the second level of hermeneutical approach towards other religions we need to make up for this deficiency caused by distancing. The phenomena exactly perceived and grasped from the distance must be described at the second level (the sign level) in their own, special context. This can be done only by participatory observation, a methodical demand which has become a matter of course in anthropological research today, but it must also be raised to the level of a *conditio sine qua non* for the academic recording of other religions and cultures.

THE PERSON STUDYING ANOTHER RELIGION	SUBJECTIVE ATTITUDE	OBJECTIVE UNDERSTANDING	LEVEL OF ACTION
1. Phenomenological level	epoché	Descriptive analysis	Perception from a distance
2. Level of signs	Sympathy	Contextualization	Participatory observation
3. Level of symbols	Empathy	Comparative interpretation	(Partial) identifycation
4. Level of relevance	a. Respect	Translation / transfer towards us	Conviviality
	b. Temptation	The question for truth is asked	Dialogue / Witness / Conviviality = mission

Whoever wants more deeply to enter into another religion and culture must take part in its rites because rites are the architecture of a religion. Its signs must, in turn, be perceived as objectively as possible, now, however, with sympathy and the will to move from the sign level into that of symbolism.

3.   The symbolism of a religion, its rites, its teachings, its practice of creating community *(Vergemeinschaftungspraxis)* must be understood on the third, the symbol level. This is only possible if you get involved in the other religion and expose yourself to its fascination — at least for a moment. This is no longer a matter of participatory observation but of 'compassionate experience'. On this level the area of experience is important, but so is the interpretation of the religion's texts. Now comparisons may — or even must — be drawn. By comparative text interpretation the symbols disclose themselves and, by such comparison which records similarity and difference, they become understandable and can be grasped, and communication becomes possible. This third level is about the inner meaning. Here religion must be seen in its totality and its inner logic must be mastered from the inside. As far as possible the other religion is perceived from the perspective of its adherents. It is indisputable that limits arise even here. However, to give up too early would mean to interrupt too soon the process of understanding. The perspective of the others, of course, is not the only valid criterion of understanding as we know from anthropology and also by semiotics. For a long time it was the only aim of text interpretation to comprehend the intention of the text with the eyes of the author; this must not be the only question. The members of an ethnic group cannot give the only authentic interpretation of their rites. Comparison with other religions can develop dimensions of symbolism which are not conscious to the participants and must be rescued from oblivion. We know that artists are not always the right and best interpreters of their own work; however, we cannot do without them. So also we cannot do without the interpretation of the members of the religion concerned. They must be able to recognize themselves in the external representation and feel themselves taken seriously.[1]

---

[1] Similar: Antes, 315

4.   With this third step both the art-historical interpretation and the academic recording of another religion come to an end.[1] Just as in matters of intercultural and inter-religious hermeneutics, we now have to enter a fourth level, the relevance level. Now the intercultural and the inter-religious hermeneutics must go their separate ways! At this level intercultural hermeneutics demand the virtue of respect; and it is its aim to make possible the peaceful living together of various cultures and the people influenced by them in such a way that every group may maintain its own integrity and yet be prepared to learn from the other one and to help the other.[2]   In interreligious hermeneutics the relevance level deals with another problem. Here the real turning point of understanding is where the other religion, with which I have been involved with sympathy and empathy, is becoming a temptation for me. A long time ago the Hamburg missiologist Prof. W. Freytag has named this as a criterion for understanding another religion. At this level one's own previous religious existence is put in question and challenged. In intercultural hermeneutics aesthetic and ethical questions of mastering common life are concerned; religious hermeneutics, however, asks the truth question here. Everything determining my faith is placed on the test-bed. Now the other religion becomes a call, an inquiry to my own faith, an appeal to decide where I belong.

We could ask whether we are not going too far by directing such demands to hermeneutics. Non-Christian religions do not expect such a step in interreligious encounter, nor do they encourage this. On the contrary, the delimiting function of religious symbols is to preserve the members of one's own religion from strange ideas and to protect them against undesired influences and to make difficult exchanges as we can see particularly in Islam. Here we come upon a peculiarity of the Christian religion. As its nature is missionary, this religion lets itself be guided by love. Love, however, wants to understand. There is no other way for it. It has to get involved with the other one, even if it thereby risks itself. And Ch.-H. Ratschow was quite right also to refer to another point: The Christian faith is fundamentally a faith which is always contested. In view of the unfathomable reality of God and in

---

[1] Cf. Panofsky; Van Straten.
[2] In detail: Sundermeier l.c., 155ff. and 183 ff.

view of the reality of our world and that of the other religion, Christian faith is always a contested faith. This is the reason for its vulnerability.[1] But this can also be seen as its strength. Its kenotic structure (Philippians 2) belongs to the nature of the Christian faith. It must abandon itself if it wants to be itself, and has to get deeply involved with the other religion. As Paul says: for Jews become a Jew, for Gentiles become a Gentile. This is the reason why missionaries have brought such progress to the methodology of 'understanding the research of religions' and have tried to understand other religions from inside. They have presented them in a way that readers occasionally doubt whether in view of the beauty and depth of the described religions one should really act as a missionary. The object of mission, of the meeting of the church with other religions, is not the meeting of a superior religion with an inferior one but with truth. The answering of the truth question can, however, only be undertaken within the horizon of understanding. Inter-religious hermeneutics serve to create the sphere of understanding. In that way they enable both pure and honourable dialogue and mutual witness to the truth which is believed and determinative for one's own life. In this encounter, as R. Otto says, "political systems, economic groups, social interests ... do not act against each other" but finally "spirit will meet spirit, ideal will meet ideal, experience will meet experience, everybody will have to tell, without cover, what deepest, what sincere truth they have and whether they have anything at all".[2]

Only on this basis can different religions live together, thus serving peace, the most important gift of the coming kingdom, the Kingdom of God.

References

Peter Antes, *Theologie und Religionswissenschaft. Methodische Anmerkungen zu Nähe und Distanz*, in: Wege der Wege der

---

[1] Cf. Margull.
[2] Otto, 155.

Theologie: an der Schwelle zum 3. Jahrtausend (FS H. Waldenfels), Paderborn, 1996, 313-324.

Hans-Joachim Margull, *Verwundbarkeit und Bemerkungen zum Dialog*, in: EvTh, 1974, 410-420.

Rudolf Otto, *Vishnu-Narayana*, Jena, 1917, 155.

Erwin Panofsky, *Zum Problem der Beschreibung und Inhaltsdeutung von Werken der bildenden Kunst*, in: Logos, 1932, 103-119.

Carl Heinz Ratschow, Der angefochtene Glaube, Gütersloh, [5]1983.

Georg Simmel, *Soziologie. Untersuchungen über die Formen der Vergesellschaftung*. Berlin, [6]1983 (1908).

Roelof van Straten, *Einführung in die Ikonographie*, Berlin, 1989.

Theo Sundermeier, *Den Fremden verstehen. Eine praktische Hermeneutik*, Göttingen, 1996.

Benedict Schubert – Photo: Waltz/EMS

Emmanuel Kwame Tettey – Photo: Sambo/EMS

Lessons learned from the Basel Mission's History –
A Personal Account

Benedict Schubert

Dear friends, colleagues, brothers and sisters,

In their invitation, the conveners of this Symposium asked me to draw upon the Basel Mission heritage. I should do so by telling stories, should show how and where I and we can still learn from these forefathers and foremothers – and, on top of everything else, show links to the Reformation. Fortunately, those conveners also asked for a relaxed presentation. However, you will understand that the task did not leave me too relaxed while preparing.

In the following, I will present a few loosely-connected examples of actions and decisions taken by persons in the orbit of the Basel Mission. I will show you how they speak to me, and hopefully to you as well, as you go about doing mission. Don't expect, in other words, a clearly-structured analysis, but a rather personal testimony. I've also been asked to make use of my musical abilities. These are limited. But after all, one gift of the Spirit may well be the ability to be imperfect. Accordingly, I'll be inviting you to join me in the singing at some points.

Allow me to start with my own story. The Basel Mission was, from my earliest childhood, part and parcel of the furniture in my world. I heard stories of my grandfather's brother, who had served and been killed as a missionary in Borneo, now known as Kalimantan. My father was the pastor of a church in a Basel suburb. But there too, the Basel Mission was present. When I went to Sunday School, I placed my offertory coin in a slit in a small collection box. On the top of that box was the image of a small African boy kneeling, his hands folded. A mechanism made the boy nod his head gratefully as soon as the coin fell into the box. The caption read: "I am a small heathen boy, yet I know my Saviour. Therefore, I beg you: take care of this poor heathen." The first song I learned in a non-European language was "Bani ngeti Ba Yawe – Let us praise the Lord our God – a song from Cameroon. There were "Mission Fairs" where people sold fruits, baked goods, books and hand-knit sweaters to support the work of the Basel Mission. I can't even recall the first time I entered the "Missionshaus", that impressive, at the time rather dark building with its strange smell on the Missionsstrasse – the "Mission Street", as it is called to this day.

It never crossed my mind, however, that I myself would become a part of the mission over and beyond the European context.. My wife and I did – together with friends – found a community, the purpose of which was to find creative ways of getting people in touch with the Gospel, with faith, with Christ. But our aim was to reach out to people in Switzerland and Germany, not beyond. It is true that for almost thirty years, this group has maintained a special relationship to the Moravians, going back to the time when it took over their girls' school near Neuchâtel, turning it into a retreat center.

But be that as it may, mission beyond the European context was not part of my intentions. The internationality of my own family was enough for me: My paternal grandparents were German, my maternal grandmother Dutch. The only Swiss among them was my maternal grandfather. Yet I fell in love with a girl from Riehen, a small town near Basel, who had grown up in Angola as the daughter of a coffee plantation owner and trader. Thanks to her, I received a letter when I was finishing up my training as pastor.

A retired missionary who had once served in Lesotho asked me – knowing that my wife was fluent in Portuguese – whether I would be willing to work in Angola as a pastor and a teacher. Since learning Portuguese was a must, and Angola itself was engulfed in civil war, the job was not exactly what you would call attractive. But for us, it was, and after spending half a year in Lisbon learning Portuguese, I lived and worked – with my growing family – for almost nine years in Luanda, pastoring in the slums of the city and training Angolan community leaders and future pastors. The civil war prevented us from staying any longer. We returned to Switzerland. I did a doctorate and took over a specialized ministry in my home church in Basel promoting mission in international solidarity in the congregations of our region. It was during this time that I became a regular visitor at the "Missionshaus". Then, in 2002, the newly founded "mission 21" recruited me as an instructor, meaning that I took office in the

Missionshaus, and became increasingly acquainted with its treasures and heritage. My focus on Africa lost its predominance. I had the opportunity to travel to China, to organize a Conference on "Peace Resources in the Religious Traditions of Bali", to conduct study trips for students to Indonesia and Cameroon and to make two visits to Latin America. My international contacts widened, as did my horizon.

Then, in 2010, I took on pastoral responsibilities at St. Peter's, an old church in the center of Basel with a long and devoted tradition, yet struggling with the specific problems all Churches must deal with in Western Europe, particularly in the cities. Sometimes, I say, jokingly, that I have become a "missionary" again. And, to be honest, it is not a joke.

Besides being pastor at St. Peter's, my wife and I are responsible for a student's dormitory, home for some 25 young people coming from various academic disciplines and very different backgrounds. By the way: we now have a student from Indonesia in our community. Should in one of your own Churches someone plan to study or do academic research at the University of Basel, do let us know. We might have the possibility of hosting that person.

The last important turn in our biography was the arrival of two refugees from Afghanistan, two brothers from Herat, 14 and 17 years old, who joined our family 1 ½ years ago.

It is, thus, from this perspective that I speak to you.

Welcome Table

I'm gonna sit at the welcome table
I'm gonna sit at the welcome table,
one of these days.
I'm gonna sit at the welcome table
Sit at the welcome table one of these days.

I'm gonna feast on milk and honey…
I'm gonna tell God how you treat me…
All God's children gonna sit together…

I start with this song. It is inspired by one of the main biblical metaphors for God's future: We'll be sitting at a heavenly banquet. The dishes might not be exactly those we know and love from our upbringing, but we'll delight in them and in each other's presence. We'll remember all the good they have done to us – and all the blessings we received from God. We'll celebrate diversity as the gift given by a Creator full of imagination. "God will wipe every tear from their eyes. Death will be no more; mourning and crying and pain will be no more, for the first things have passed away." (Revelations 21:4)

There have always been two basic motivations for mission. The one is dramatic, apocalyptic: human beings are seen drowning in the sea of damnation, mission being the challenge of drawing them into the life boat, that is the community of true believers. Time is short, the end is near. The other is brighter: we are drawn towards God's future. He has "plans for your welfare and not for harm, to give you a future with hope." (Jeremiah 29:11)

Even though the Basel Mission and its agents may have sometimes given a bleak picture of how the "heathen world" was lost – the overall impression I gained from Basel is that her core motivation was to better the living conditions of those to which her missionaries were sent.

This makes all the difference: whether the basic emotion is fear or hope.

…and set God's people free

Lydia Ndamboked, a young woman of noble blood, arrived at the royal court of Fumban in Cameroon shortly before WW1 begun. She became a mistress of the king. When the first missionaries came to Fumban, she heard and accepted with the Gospel, including the missionaries' understanding of marriage. She then decided not to be a mistress any longer, asking to be married instead. This she was, to a high-ranking member of the court, the royal chamberlain. Her husband adored her abilities, her skills, her graciousness, but he soon realized that her new belief called the traditional foundations of their society into question. Afraid that she might contribute to the subversion of the social and political order, he had her tortured. Anna

Wuhrmann, famous missionary and photographer, wrote that she "suffered severely".

Lydia Ndamboked. Photo: BMA

The two women became close friends and allies. When Anna Wuhrmann had to leave the country because of the war in 1915, she worried about the fate of Lydia. However, when Anna returned, in 1920, Lydia was there with other women, cheering and greeting her. During the missionaries' absence, the Christian community had grown and Lydia was its heart and soul. Anna Wuhrmann reported: "There was a great stir when the most influential Christians named Lydia a 'congregational elder'. It was unheard of! A woman in the council of men! With full voting rights! A woman, of which one otherwise hears with contempt: 'Just a female.'"

I came across Lydia Ndamboked when I read the book published for the Basel Mission Jubilee two years ago. I do not know more about her than what I have told you here. I hold up her example because I see in it that which is to my mind the most important element in mission:

Those involved in the mission of Christ are no doubt marked by their ambivalent attitudes, convictions, prejudices and assumptions. Yet the liberating force of the Gospel finds its way to transforming individual and social lives.

"The Lord is the Spirit, and where the Spirit of the Lord is, there is freedom." (2 Cor 3:16). God's Spirit is a Spirit which sets people free

– and in doing so, the Spirit sometimes goes against the will of those who act in her name to proclaim the Gospel.

Missionaries went to the places of their mission with the intention of bringing about change. In retrospect, we can see that the changes they wanted to bring about were unnecessary or even problematic – yet the Spirit had its own subversive energy, like an undercurrent.

While I was in Angola trying to learn the local language Kikongo, I once asked my teacher, an elderly, very friendly Angolan, how he saw the missionaries' legacy. He answered: "There was probably no need to destroy so much of our traditional culture. All the same, they brought us the Gospel, and we cannot be grateful enough for this."

In a short text on "God's action in History" (from his "letters from prison"), Bonhoeffer once stated: "I believe that even our errors and mistakes are turned to good account. It is no harder for God to cope with them than with what we imagine to be our good deeds."

***

> *If you believe and I believe*
> *and we together pray,*
> *the Holy Spirit must come down*
> *and set God's people free,*
> *and set God's people free,*
> *and set God's people free.*
> *The Holy Spirit must come down*
> *and set God's people free.*

The song came from revivalist sources in Britain and was translated into various African languages. The original text goes:

> *He did not come to judge the world,*
> *He did not come to blame,*
> *He did not only come to seek,*
> *it was to save He came.*
> *And when we call Him Saviour,*
> *and when we call Him Saviour,*
> *and when we call Him Saviour,*
> *then we call Him by His name.*

In the world, but not belonging to the world

A friend of one of my sons asked me one day whether I knew something about her grand-grandfather Gottfried Zürcher. Her own family knew only that he had been a Basel Missionary. Upon finding the name to be included in the index of the five-volume "History of the Basel Mission" I proceeded to consult his personal file in the Basel Mission Archives.

Gold Coast Missionaries 1909; 1st from right: Gottfried Zürcher.

Photo: BMA

Gottfried Zürcher was sent to the Gold Coast (now Ghana) as missionary at the turn of the last century. He went with his wife; they had four children. Sadly, his wife died. He then married a female missionary who was already stationed in the Gold Coast; together, they had another five children. Shortly before World War I broke out, the Zürchers had been on home leave. They returned to Christiansborg just before the war broke out, and Gottfried was promoted to the office of Basel Mission "Field Secretary".

When the war started, the first reaction of the colonial authorities was friendly and pragmatic. Deputy Governor Robertson acknowledged the merits of the missionaries, the friendships across nationalities and the needs of the population. However, the tone soon changed, a first low point being reached when Kaundinya, a clerk of the "Basel Mission Trading Company" was arrested. He was charged with having given signals to German cruiser at sea, though he himself claimed to have only been collecting shells at the sea shore. Kaundinya was held in captivity in Accra for two years before being deported to England in November 1916. The irony of this was that the first member of the Basel Mission community to be arrested was a British-Indian citizen, the son of the first Indian to be sent to Basel for missionary training. Hermann Anand Kaundinya, the father of the unfortunate "Kaundinya", was himself of Brahmin lineage. Convinced of the truth of the Gospel, he converted to Christianity, though he continued to hold his traditional faith and philosophy in high esteem. During his training in Switzerland, he married the daughter of a Wuerttemberg pastor. He was subsequently ordained as a missionary in Germany.

Basel Mission Trading Company and staff in Accra 1900; 3rd from left: Hermann Kaundinya. Photo: BMA

It was thus his son who was the first to be arrested. The Basel "Committee" tried to avoid further damage and to assure the continuation of the work. Secret talks were held with the Church of Scotland and her mission board. Nevertheless, all German missionaries were deported in November 1917, and in February 1918, even the remaining Swiss were expelled – even though they protested on the grounds of Swiss neutrality.

In Gottfried Zürcher's file, I found a touching postcard he wrote from London while on his way back to Switzerland. No complaints, only very discreet allusions to the difficulties, but deep gratitude for God's guidance and protection.

I tell you this story not only because it illustrates how common it is to find in Swiss Protestant families an ancestor who was linked to the Basel Mission, which again shows how deeply-rooted the Basel Mission was in Swiss Society. I choose this story for another reason.

I chose it because it shows how closely mission history and world history are intertwined. There is, understandably, an inclination to simplify the relationship between Colonial dominance and exploitation on the one hand and Christian mission on the other. There are those who never cease to emphasize that mission was nothing more than the religious component of the colonial conquest of the world, a sort of religious imperialism. And then there are the mission apologetics, who insist that mission was and is a counter-force to colonial oppression.

Both views are too simplistic. You will find, needless to say, anecdotal illustrations for both. Yet we cannot avoid the difficult task of looking closely at the different situations in the context of their time. Further, we must bear in mind the key difference between a moral critique and a moral judgment.

Jesus, in His famous prayer for his followers in John 17, states that they – the ones the Father had "given to him" – lived in a particular situation: they were in the world, but did not belong to the world.

The great mission historian Andrew F. Walls observes that Christian mission was driven by two forces or fundamental principles. One he calls the "indigenizing principle", the other the "pilgrim principle". The indigenizing force allows the Gospel to take root wherever it is proclaimed (I will return to this later when treating the issue of "translation"). It is inculturated, so that those who embrace it can feel at home in the community that is brought together by the Gospel. The other principle is the one that calls people to leave what they know and what they feel comfortable in. It is the principle that moves people to depart, to begin their journey towards God's future.

I myself believe that people committed to mission are called to let themselves be moved by both forces, remaining faithful to their calling in the midst of events over which they themselves have no control.

In doing this and living accordingly, it is of great importance – returning now to an issue taken up earlier – whether they are driven by an "apocalyptic" perspective on the world or by a "prophetic" understanding of it. In the apocalyptic perspective, we are exposed to forces far beyond our reach and control. The only option we have is to try to remain faithful. In a prophetic perspective, we believe that God's promises enable us to act in the world, to "make a difference". I say this knowing that at times, Christians necessarily find themselves in situations that are "apocalyptic", meaning that they are like pawns in a game played by seemingly supernatural and demonic forces.

Devotion

Photo: private

During a study tour in 2008, the group, of which I was a member, visited one of the great mosques in Banjarmasin / Kalimantan. An elderly man showed us around. At the end of the visit, I told him that I had personal links to Banjarmasin, as my grand-uncle had once served here as a missionary doctor. "Dr. Vischer? I knew him. When I was a child, he once gave me a lesson on hygiene." It was very moving for me to meet someone who had actually met the man who was a mythic figure in my own family history.

Matthaeus & Betsy Vischer-Mylius were sent to what was then called Borneo in 1927. Before Matthaeus could start working as a doctor, he had to organize the construction of the hospital and the house for himself and his family in Kuala Kapuas. He succeeded at both tasks and went on to construct a leprosy station and to institute a training school for nurses and midwives.

Photo: BMA

When World War II began, all German missionaries were brought to internment camps by the Dutch. But not the Vischers! They continued with their work. In the spring of 1942, the Japanese invaded Borneo. They pursued a merciless "cleansing" policy. The Vischers and other missionaries were arrested, charged with conspiracy and finally, in December 1943, shot for having participated in an anti-Japanese plot – together with 300 other victims.

The Vischers' death could most probably have been avoided. They themselves did certainly not seek martyrdom. At the same time, they did not wish to prioritize their own well-being over that of their mission.

"Martyrdom" has been in recent times perverted. We are aware of the danger of people being seduced into wasting their lives, throwing the gift of God away for something worthless – deaths that are not a testimony of love, but of hatred or simple stupidity.

The famous story of Abraham binding Isaac (Gen 22) is often told to demonstrate the depth of Abraham's faith and devotion. However, the ultimate point is that God did not want Isaac to die. His death would have been unnecessary. This is important in looking back through mission history where, sometimes, children were literally sacrificed by their devoted parents.

It is crucial that the Spirit allows us to discern whether we may be spared or be ready for a sacrifice. Jesus himself asked the Father whether he really had to drink the cup of suffering (Lk 22:42). Yet, when he knew that it could not be avoided, he took up his cross. Accordingly, as followers of Christ, there may be situations in which we, too, are called to take up and bear our cross, even if that means also that we have to lay down our lives (Mk 8:34f).

Translation

In late 1999, I had the privilege to accompany Ernst Itten on a visit to the congregations of the Church in the Guandong Province in Southern China. Itten had been a missionary to China before the Revolution. Throughout his subsequent ministry as a pastor in the Berne region of Switzerland, the Hakka people occupied a special place in his heart. As soon as the political situation allowed, he began returning to China for visits. He toured the villages preaching and teaching in perfect Hakka, yet with a heavy Bernese accent. It was fascinating to be with him.

One evening in Laolung (the photo below dates from before World War II), Ernst had already gone to sleep. I was sitting in the living room with P. Tong, my local colleague. He spoke several Chinese languages, I speak some European ones – but we had no language in common. I don't remember why – but suddenly, he started humming tune and we started singing. I knew the song only in Portuguese and

Kikongo. It is one of the hymns sung in many Churches around the world.

Laolung; Photo: BMA

This experience led me to reflect more thoroughly on mission as a translation movement. Luke relates the story of Pentecost as a miracle of communication: people from different origins and languages all hear those who had been overwhelmed by the Spirit speaking of God's wonderful deeds "in their own languages". (Act 2:6.8.11!)

The missionaries did sometimes consider it imperative that their addressees adopt their cultural norms and habits – a mistake, as we can see in hindsight. But they never forgot that the Gospel wants to reach all people in their own languages. One of the first tasks undertaken was that of translating the Bible into the vernacular. This gave rise to a reversal of the power structures – sometimes contrary to the missionaries' intention. Those for whom the "vernacular" was their mother tongue always had an advantage. They became teachers – even though some missionaries considered them to be "children". Moreover, the translated text was enriched with additional meaning. The Gospel became, so to say, wider. Translating the message continues to be a challenge, and it could well be that our Churches in Europe must now "retranslate" it to render it understandable in the present society with its different cultural milieus.

A - 30. 9. 30

Bible translators, Hongkong, ca. 1900; Photo: BMA

The missionaries not only translated the Bible, but also hymns, or more precisely their lyrics. This has an interesting effect. When a biblical text is translated into another language, only those who know that language are able to read and understand it. If that language uses an alphabet I myself am not familiar with, I cannot even recognize it for what it is – a biblical text.

If a hymn is translated into and sung in another language, I may still recognize it. The tune allows me to feel at home, even if the language is totally foreign to me. I remember a Sunday in Denpasar, Bali. We were preparing a Conference. In the morning, I wanted to attend a local Church service, even though I don't speak the language. I sat in the congregation, not understanding a word until the singing began. Two of the songs came from that treasure of hymns that have been spread around the world. Singing gave me the feeling of belonging. I had known it in my head: I knew I was in a Church, I recognized the signs and symbols. But only when I could sing along did I feel in my heart, not only in my head, that I was part of this body. Maybe hymns fulfill, for our Protestant Churches, the function the universal liturgy of the Mass has for our Catholic brothers and sisters.

By translating and in particular by translating hymns, the Basel Mission has made an invaluable contribution to the worldwide Church as a "unity in diversity". This not only by translating, as in the 19th century, Western hymns into various vernaculars, but also by translating, now in the 21st, hymns and choruses from all over the world.

References

These are the books (in English) that have influenced me most in my reflections on mission and in preparing this presentation:

Basler Mission / EMW (Hg.), *Thuma Mina. Internationales Ökumenisches Liederbuch. International Ecumenical Hymnbook*, Basel u.a. 1995

Stephen B. Bevans / Roger P. Schroeder, *Constants in Context. A Theology of Mission for Today*, Maryknoll 2004

David Bosch, *Transforming Mission. Paradigm Shifts in Theology of Mission*, Maryknoll 1993

Dietrich Bonhoeffer, *Letters & Papers from Prison*, New York 1997.

Christine Christ-von Wedel / Thomas Kuhn, *Basel Mission. People, History, Perspectives 1815-2015*, Basel 2015

Sebastian Kim / Kirsteen Kim, *Christianity as a World Religion*, London / New York 2008

Lamin Sanneh, *Translating the Message. The Missionary Impact on Culture*, Maryknoll 1990

Andrew F. Walls, *The Missionary Movement in History. Studies in the Transmission of Faith*, Maryknoll 1997

Andrew F. Walls, *The Cross-Cultural Process in Christian History. Studies in the Transmission and Appropriation of Faith*, Maryknoll 2002

Andrew F. Walls / Cathy Ross (Hg), *Mission in the Twenty-First Century. Exploring the Five Marks of Global Mission*, Maryknoll 2008

Brian Wren, *Praying Twice. The Music and Words of Congregational Song*, Louisville KY 2000

Pictures from the Basel Mission Archives:

P. 51: BMA, Ref. Nr. E-30.30.004 „King's daughter Lydia Ndamboked"

P. 53: BMA, Ref. Nr. D-30.20.002 "Goldküste Missionare: Groh, W. Rottmann, Dr. Fisch, Bellon, Josenhans, Zürcher"

P. 54: BMA, Ref. Nr. QU-30.003.0020 „BMF Agent und Staff in Accra. Berger, Blattmann, Brugger, Kaundinya, Giezendanner, Roesle, Back, Frau & Herr Binhammer"

P. 57: BMA, Ref. Nr. B-30.65.122 „Herr u. Frau Vischer mit Schwester M. Hoersch…"

P. 59: BMA, Ref. Nr. QA-30.004.0125 „Station Laolung"

P. 60: BMA, Ref. Nr. A-30.09.030 „Bibelübersetzer in Hongkong"

Sankofa: The Relevance of Our Missionary Roots

Emmanuel Kwame Tettey

Introduction

The topic for my presentation is supposed to be *'The Relevance of Our Roots'*. In my country Ghana, there is somethings called *adinkra* symbols. These are symbols which represent concepts as well as some values, ideals, and aspirations of the society. One of these symbols is the *sankofa*. *Sankofa* literary means "return and get it". The *sankofa* symbol portrays the importance of learning from the past. It inspires courage to revisit our past. I guess this is what we intend to do with the given topic so permit me to reframe my topic to read: *"Sankofa: The Relevance of Our Missionary Roots."*

Our root is our past, and our heritage. Our roots are our history, the context and the people who moved that history. Some stories of the past may be pleasant and others unpleasant. But whatever the case may be, from our roots, heritage and our past, we bring a luggage of lessons. Discussing the relevance of our roots demands that we examine both the negative and positive aspects of our past and look at what lessons we can apply for today. This is exactly what I will attempt to do in this presentation. Our roots, in this context, is the work of the Basel Missionaries particularly in the Gold Coast.

From the time the first Basel Missionary arrived in the Gold Coast till the day the last foreign missionary left, there are several lessons of courage, persistence, faith and spiritual discipline among others that we can learn for our Christian mission today. In this presentation, however, I will focus on selected events and developments during the work of the Basel Missionaries in Ghana (then Gold Coast) and discuss them in line with what I believe is the most significant lesson relevant for Christian mission today.

As Christians, our missionary roots go beyond the Basel Missionaries or any other human missionary group in history. In 1 Corinthians 3:11, we read that: *"For no one can lay any foundation other than the one that has been laid; that foundation is Jesus Christ."* (NSRV).

Whatever our missionary history may be, that history is also rooted in our Lord Jesus Christ, the Word of God. I would therefore request that you permit me to discuss the activities of the Basel Missionaries alongside some similar Biblical events in order to enhance the understanding of the points I intend to make.

The King's Challenge

The history books tell us that the first batch of four Basel missionaries arrived in the Gold Coast (modern Ghana) on 18th December 1828 at the request of the then Danish government which was colonizing the West African country at the time. In about eight months, three (3) of these missionaries died and by 1831, the fourth person also died.

The Mission Society in Basel was not discouraged by the demise of these three missionaries. They sent another batch of three missionaries to continue the work. This time there was a medical doctor among the three, probably to take care of their health to prevent the early death recorded among the first batch. Interestingly, Dr. Heinze rather died first within six (6) week. The second person also died and only Andreas Riis survived. In March 1835, Andreas Riis decided to move from the coastal part of the Gold Coast to a mountainous area called Akropong. Riis stayed in Akropong until 1840 when he had to go back to Basel with the wife for a leave. Up till this time, there was no convert.[1]

Before departing the Gold Coast, Riis went to the Akuapem King to say goodbye. In their farewell discussion, the King, Nana Addo Dankwa I threw a challenge to Andreas Riis. The King posed the challenge in the following words:

"When God created the world, he made the Book for the Whiteman and the juju (fetish) for the Blackman. If you can show us some Blackman, who can read the Whiteman's book (the Bible), then we would surely follow you."[2]

---

[1] Nkansah-Kyeremateng, 42.
[2] Schweizer, 50-51. Also Nkansah-Kyeremateng, 44.

Upon arrival in Switzerland, Riis carried the information on the King's challenge to the Home Committee of the Basel Mission Society. Schweizer reports that the Basel Mission in Switzerland received the news as an encouraging opportunity to give the mission one more chance.[1] Riis and others were dispatched to Jamaica to bring some black Moravians to the Gold Coast in response to the King's challenge. Six families and three other persons were brought from Jamaica and that was the key that opened the heart of the people of the Gold Coast to receive the gospel. [2]

The questions or the challenge posed by the chief may sound cynical or sarcastic or even racist and could have been dismissed but when it was responded to, it ended up to be the key that opened up the community to Christ. Today, many people are asking similar questions and posing similar challenges to our Christian mission.

One of my surprises when I first stayed in Germany for my voluntary work was the fact that many people, especially the youth, have little interest in the Church. So I decided to conduct a survey on why the youth are not interested in the Church. It wasn't a scientific survey though. Anytime I met any young person, I asked them what puts them away from the Church. One of them interestingly told me that *"Emmanuel, I love to dance so I go to disco on Saturdays and come home late. I am therefore not able to wake up early to go to Church on Sunday."* He added that *"may be if the Church service gives me the opportunity to dance, I would consider it"* (paraphrasing). As far as this statement is concerned, this young person is not any different from the 19th century Nana Addo Dankwa I of the Gold Coast.

I also do hear a lot of people ask, and I do ask too, that how is it that in many African countries, there are majority Christians yet vices such as corruption and conflicts continue to persist? Where then lies the relevance of the Church?

The experience of the Basel Mission with the challenge of the Akuapem King teaches us that in our missionary activities, it is important to listen to questions being asked by the people and help

---

[1] Schweizer, 51.
[2] Nkansah-Kyeremateng, 44.

them find answers in Christ. Instead of setting off with ready-made solutions, we may be more effective when we listen to the people. The early Apostles employed this methodology too as manifested in the book of Acts. In our Christian mission, it is necessary to engage people at the level where they are not the level where we are.

Schools and Mother Tongue Usage

The records also tell us that a major priority of the Basel Missionaries was to master the local languages so they could speak to the people in a language they understood.[1] This agenda was indeed religiously pursued. The missionaries did learn some of the local languages and it may be amazing to note that Johannes Zimmerman, a German missionary for instance, studied the Ga language and played a leading role in translating the Bible into the Ga local language. Johannes Christaller, another Basel missionary also worked with some indigenes to translate the bible into the Twi language.

That wasn't all! The Basel Missionaries established seminaries and trained the indigenous people in indigenous languages. One writer, Iheanacho, gave a testimony of this initiative saying:

"The Seminary products were therefore enabled to teach not only successive students, but also to explain otherwise difficult concepts like 'salvation', 'atonement' or justification' to seekers, converts and others in their own mother tongue. As a result, the Gospel and the culture engagement could take place through the medium of the indigenous languages."[2]

Translation as the Essence of Mission

I am sure by now, you would have realized from the stories told so far, that there were conscious efforts on the part of the Basel Missionaries to enable the people of the Gold Coast to see and appreciate God's love and salvation within their own context. That is translation! I

---

[1] Iheanacho, 28.
[2] Iheanacho, 12.

believe the most important lesson we can learn from our roots, the Basel Mission is the need to approach Christian mission as an act of translation.

Translation is basically about transferring meaning from one language (the source language) to another language called the receptor language.

Translation is divine and very essential for our Christian faith. As Andrew Walls would put it, the "Christian faith rest on a divine act of translation".[1] Indeed, "God chose translation as a mode of action for the salvation of humanity".[2] Our Lord Jesus Christ, who is also our master missionary root beyond the Basel Missionaries, is very instrumental in God's act of translation. In Jesus Christ, God transferred meaning from divinity to humanity as "the Word became fresh, and dwelt among us" (John 1:14).

Interestingly, we are having this conversation during a Pentecost period. In Acts 2 where we find the Pentecost story was the manifestation of the power of the Holy Spirit. We also say that the event which occurred during Pentecost was the birth of the Church. The fact that the immediate manifestation of the Holy Spirit among the Apostles was to speak new different languages of the people around was an indication of the God's empowerment to the Church to engage in translation of the Gospel.

Translation as demonstrated by God through Jesus Christ is the divine generic mission strategy which the Basel Missionaries attempted to exemplify. And this is what I wish to highlight as relevance of our roots for Christian mission today.

Again, from the example of Jesus Christ, we realize that translation is not only about linguistics. It is most importantly about transferring an original meaning from one context into another context. In our case, it would involve how to help:

- That rich man or woman who thinks he doesn't need God to realize that it is the same God who gives riches and can take it back at any time.

---

[1] Wall, 26.
[2] Ibid.

- That oppressed person who thinks God is not just to appreciate that God in interested in his or her wellbeing.
- That 21st century young man or woman who sees not the relevance of having a relationship with Jesus Christ and fellowship with other believers to appreciate that life is not only about what we experience now.

The famous Scottish missiologists, Prof. Andrew F. Walls was once asked why the Church in the West is going down and he said "because they have stopped translating". If you ask me of the greatest weakness of the Church in Africa, I would say "it is inadequate and improper translation".

The application of the principle of translation in our Christian mission today may practically not be that easy. I however wish to suggest some four (4) practical ways that we can do this:

1.   *Cultural Sensitivity and Dynamism in Mission*

We have to be dynamic in our Christian ministry and missionary approach. We also have to be sensitive to the interest, culture and sub-cultures of not only communities and ethnic groups but also to the various generations in the "mission field".

The story of the encounter between the Jews and the Gentiles and the eventual verdict of the Apostolic Council as recorded in Acts 15 reminds us that it is always possible for us to confuse the essentials of the Christian Faith with our traditions and conventional practices which are sometimes associated with our culture and exigencies of the time. I think it is in this area that the work of the Basel missionaries in the Gold Coast has been quite confining for the mission then and the Church today. Examples abound!

From the European tradition, anyone who stands in the pulpit to preach must usually be dressed in the cassock or a suit. Something interesting happened in the PCG in 1931. One young man by name Ephraim Amu was given the opportunity to preach in Church. Contrary to the conventional costume for the pulpit, Ephraim Amu chose to preach dressed in a cloth wrapped around his body, a traditional Ghanaian style of dressing. This was considered by the Church leadership then to be a great offence and for his punishment, Ephraim Amu was banned from preaching. In fact, he was later dismissed from the Presbyterian Training College and seminary where he was training to become a teacher. [1]

Of course, if you are familiar with the timelines, you would realize that by 1931, the Basel Missionaries were not in charge in the then Gold Coast at the time that Ephraim Amu was dismissed. But it is clear that the thinking behind Amu's dismissal is an offshoot of the Basel Missionaries' rigidity and strict adherence to guidelines concerning doctrine, liturgy and prescribed conducts of missionaries, Church members and leaders. The strict implementation of the *Hausordnung* to regulate the lives of the trainees in the seminary in Basel was extended to the Gold Coast. David Kpobi reports that the missionaries had instructions covering every detailed live of the missionaries including even "the make-up of a proper missionary wardrobe... the daily allowance of wine, the quantity and style of home furnishing" and even the kind of woman to get married with.[2] Johannes Zimmermann, for instance, was handed a very severe punishment of losing his European citizenship for insisting on marrying Catherine, an African, without the approval of the Home Committee in Basel.

There was no room for flexibility with some practices which were in actual sense not necessarily essential to the faith yet inconsistent with or alien to the worldview of the indigenous people.

Prof. Patrick. L. O. Lunumba was right when he observed during a lecture he delivered in Ghana that for Africans, when we are sad, we dance and when we are happy too we dance. In the African traditional society and primal religion, singing and dancing means a lot and very central to worshiping of the deities. It was therefore strange for the local people to come before the Supreme God in Church and only stand in an attention mood to sing hymns without drums, clapping and dancing. Unfortunately, this was how the Basel Mission instituted worship services were and continued even when the Church was led

---

[1] Laryea, 19.
[2] Kpobi, 17.

by indigenous people. Until some few decades ago, clapping, drumming and dancing was not allowed in the Presbyterian Church of Ghana as a legacy handed down by the Basel and other missionaries. This definitely would make a typical African at the time sceptical of the Christian faith.

The point is, even though the Basel Mission did very well in addressing the linguistic needs of the people, in the twin category of being sensitive to the culture of the people and openness to change, especially with regard to liturgy and Christian practices, the Basel mission was lacking. Christian Mission as an act of translation is not only about the language. It is also about being attentive to the culture of the people and responding appropriately. This also means that in our missionary activities, we must be open to change because the culture and sub-culture of people groups change over time. We have to be willing to change our approach and ways of doing things if that change is not about the essentials of the faith. Approaching Christian mission as an act of translation initiated by God means that reformation must be continuous.

For example, we understand our liturgy to be a chosen style of how to express our faith based on our understanding of what God expects of us. We, however, have to be concerned about how our chosen style of worship, for instance, draws people to or puts people away from faith in our Lord Jesus Christ. We should not find it to be radical to seek to change when it becomes necessary. I see this to be a challenge for the mission of the Church in Europe but also in other parts of the world including my own country.

As a descendant of the Basel mission, the Presbyterian Church of Ghana was negatively affected as it also found it difficult to respond to contextual changes quick enough to address the cultural needs of the people. As a result, many of the PCG members had to leave to join the charismatic Churches as they found the charismatic movement to be more responsive to their spiritual needs given their primal religious background. We thank God that the situation now keeps improving.

So the lesson here, from the work of the Basel Missionaries, is that the Church, as a matter of necessity, must have a dogma but the Church needs not to be dogmatic in the way it puts the dogma into practice.

The Basel mission experience teaches us that if we are to succeed in approaching mission as a translation movement then we have to be sensitive to the culture, sub-culture, interest and concerns of the communities, the generations and the people whom we reach out to.

2. *Seek Knowledge of Other Faiths*

Some believers hold the view that seeking to know of other faiths is a waste of time. However, conveying meaning from one context to the other demands that one is familiar with both contexts. The more the Basel missionaries got to know and understand the belief systems of the people of the Gold Coast, the more effective they were.

In his witness to the people in Athens as recorded in Acts 17, our ancestor and elder brother Apostle Paul was effective, due to his demonstrated knowledge of the spirituality of the people of Athens.

Last Monday, Dr. Rima Nasrallah reminded us that in this era of plurality and the religiously branded violence we experience around us, the fear of the Church, comes up as the greatest threat to Christian mission. The fear we are referring to here is mostly based on hearsay, prejudices and stereotypes. A courageous attempt to know of the faith of others will help us overcome that fear and make us effective in translating the love of God even in this difficult times.

Dr. Kerstin Neumann told us on Tuesday that in deciding on a mission blue print for the EMS, one of the challenging questions to answer is what should be the orientation of the fellowship towards people of other faiths. Pluralism is real, and we need to respect each other and coexist peacefully. But that does not release us of the responsibility to share the Gospel with all. Refusal of a Christian to share the good news is, in my opinion, selfishness and disobedience to God. Putting these two realities together puts us in a difficult situation. I think what we need to do is what we call at the Presbyterian Interfaith Research and Resource Centre, respectful and intelligent witnessing. The starting point in this, is seeking to know of the others.

3. *Deliberate Holistic Witnessing*

Translation is a deliberate and holistic enterprise that strikes a balance to give people adequate understanding and appreciation: so must our Christian mission be. We have to be deliberate in our propagation of the gospel. Yesterday we were to have some discussion on how much of evangelism must be involved in missions. I cannot imagine a mission organization or a Church that shies away from evangelism.

The Basel Missionaries in Ghana built schools and provided social service. But these were never considered to be a substitute for oral witnessing. Preaching and teaching of the Bible was a key aspect of the work of the missionaries. Even when the people seemed not to be interested, they persisted. For more than a decade, the Basel Missionaries continued to preach when nobody seemed to be interested.

For many people, they would best appreciate God's love for them when it is verbally explained to them (Romans 10: 13-17). Evangelism is especially necessary in this modern day that knowledge abounds and people continue to question the logic of the Christian Faith. We need not feel overwhelmed by the increasing level of secularism. The Basel missionaries had an equivalent context as traditional worship was very high during those days. Indeed, conviction and conversion is the work of the Holy Spirit but our participation in God's mission puts on us the indispensable responsibility to preach, teach and witness to the gospel.

In our EMS Fellowship, we commit to supporting projects in the areas of School and Vocational Education; Combating Poverty; Diakonia; Justice, Peace and Integrity of Creation; Church Education and Training; and Spreading of the Gospel. Whereas this gives us an impression of a holistic mission, there is room for improvement in the level of attention and resources committed to evangelism and spreading of the gospel in our partnerships.

4.   *Interest in the Socio-Political Space*

The Church must take interest in the socio-political space and governance of the society as a necessary missionary approach as we participate in God's mission as an act of translation. There are examples from the work of the Basel missionaries which would be useful.

During the time of the Basel Mission in the Gold Coast, the colonial government was in force but there was also a very strong local traditional governance system where the chiefs served as the political heads in their traditional jurisdictions. Each community had rules and regulations mostly in the form of taboos and folklores. Along with the political system was the traditional or primal religion with its associated beliefs and practices such as pouring of libation, animal and human sacrifices, puberty rites, widowhood rites and many other rituals.

One did not have to choose to obey these rules. It was a must for every indigene to obey these rules and abide by the practices even the religious ones. Disobedience comes with very harsh punishment. In my home town, Odumase Krobo, for instance, any lady who got pregnant before undergoing the puberty rites, Dipo, was banished from the community. Whereas some of the practices were of great social values, most of them were very unchristian, so to say. So it was a big challenge for the Christian converts and the missionaries as well. What did the Basel missionaries do?

To solve this problem, the Basel Missionaries decided to develop isolated communities or settlements for new converts so that they would not be under pressure to compromise on their new faith in Jesus Christ. These communities were called Salem. I understand that this Salem Concept was also used by the Basel Missionaries in India. To some extent it worked well.

Now, one may say that the Basel Missionaries were creative in handling the situation. Their approach has been criticized, though, to have created problems for the cohesion of the society. I would say that the Salem system was somehow confining to the Christians and the Church in the sense that it did not empower the believers to meaningfully get their new Christian faith to interact with the traditional culture beliefs and practices. But for missionary purposes, the approach by the Basel missionaries may be justifiable since they could not do anything about the traditional political system.

Fast forward to the 21st century, are we facing similar situation? I would say yes except that the details are not the same. In our days, it is getting more difficult to separate religion from politics. This is especially so with the increasing levels of religious extremism and radicalization used for political purposes. States and governments continue to take decision, enact laws and initiate policies which limit the progress of religion in general and Christianity in particular.

Our brothers and sisters in Indonesia are struggling to deal with the infamous blasphemy law; brethren in India are contending with state-backed radical Hinduist and the insurgence of political Islam in Asia, the Middle East and Africa remain a threat. The increasing pressure to satisfy the insatiable demand for human freedom and right is pushing governments in Europe, America and elsewhere to implement policies that provide grounds for secularism to foster.

It is true that people's religious commitment is a function of their social, economic and political context. The good news is that the converse is also true: religion has the potential to influence the social, political and economic context. If this were not possible, our Lord Jesus probably may not have told us that we are the salt and light of the earth. He tells us that we should make disciples of "all nations". It means nations as units and not just the individuals residents of the nations.

Unlike the time of 19th century Basel Missionaries, many of our countries now have democracy. That means that we can make our voices heard and seek to influence what goes on in our society. We cannot and do not have to withdraw from the society. We have to engage those in political leadership for a society which is conducive enough for people to serve God. A church that shies away from participating in the life of the society and makes no influence on the society soon loses its salt and light nature.

I am happy that under the objective 2 of the EMS Agenda 2014-2020, as part of the EMS Focus, we commit to engage in some advocacy. I think we can empower our Member-Churches the more to address societal issues in their home countries.

Learning from the experiences of the Basel mission, we realize that participation in the socio-political space is important for Christian mission as a translation. We need to transfer meaning from the kingdom of God into the kingdom of man. What does it mean when we pray the Kingdom of God to come? What does it mean for the will of God to be done on earth as it is in heaven? These are wishes of our Lord Jesus Christ. Our Christian mission should give meaning to these words.

Conclusion

The word of God in its original language is constant. But language in itself is dynamic. It keeps changing; both the written and spoken language. The kind of German spoken in the 18th Century is not the same language Germans speak now. In the 17th Centuries, to use such expressions as 'thou', 'thee' etc. makes a very rich English but if I stand before you now or the teenagers in my Church Junior Youth group to use thee, thou, etc., they will all fall asleep because it would be boring and difficult to understand. So this is why every now and then the Bible is translated and also we see new editions of old translations to make it linguistically and practically relevant to the current generation.

In the same way, God's mission to reconcile the world to himself remains constant. But what this mission means and how it is to be done demands some variation because the contexts keep changing. This is why out of the many lessons we could learn from the work of the Basel Missionaries in Ghana, the then Gold Coast, I wish to recommend the concept of translation. That we approach our Christian mission as a translation movement.

Our society and our world has seen interesting developments:

- We are in an era in which materialism, secularism and atheism are gaining prominences.
- We are being overwhelmed by fundamentalism and extremism.

- Our human freedom is put ahead of, over and above human responsibility towards God.
- The gap between faith and practice keeps widening.

As dynamic and interesting as our society has become, the context of our world will continue to change but our call to mission remains constant. In spite of these changes, God's expectation of us to actively participate in His mission remains constant. This means that we have to constantly examine the cultural, political, legal, technological and economic changes in our environment and ask for the guidance of the Holy Spirit on how to translate the meaning of the love of God for the understanding of peoples of all generations and culture such that as many people as possible shall come to have faith and benefit from the saving power of our Lord Jesus Christ. This is a lesson from our roots.

It is not going to be easy but we must always remember that *"it is not by might nor by power but by the Spirit of the Lord"*. Thank you.

References

Iheanacho, Maureen O., *Theophilus Opoku – Indigenous Pastor and Missionary Theologian, 1842-1913*, Sahara Publishers, Accra, 2014.

Kpobi, David N. A., *Mission and Governance: The Evolution of Practices and Procedures of the Presbyterian Church of Ghana*, Waterville Publishing, Accra, 2011.

Laryea, Philip T., *Ephraim Amu: Nationalist, Poet and Theologian*, Regnum Africa, Akropong, 2012.

Nkansah-Kyeremateng, K., *The Presbyterian Church of Ghana: History and Impact,* Sebewie Publishers, Accra, 2003.

Schweizer, Peter A., *Survivors on the Gold Coast: The Basel Missionaries in Colonial Ghana*, Smart Publishing, Accra, 2000.

Wall, Andrew F., *The Missionary Movement in Christian History: Studies in the Transmission of Faith*, Orbis Books, Maryknoll, 1996.

PART 2: FROM THE TEAM VISIT REPORTS

At its meeting in November 2014, the EMS General Meeting confirmed a resolution taken by the Mission Council one year earlier, recommending that the EMS Secretariat would conduct a series of Team Visits in order *to 'mirror' the differing understandings and practices of mission in the churches and missions of the EMS Fellowship and also of churches which are linked to Basel Mission German Branch.* It was agreed that four such visits would take place, the hosting churches being in Ghana, India, Indonesia and Germany. The teams themselves would be international in composition, their members being nominated by their respective churches or mission organizations. These Teams would not be composed of persons who already knew the hosting churches well. The idea was rather to look for first impressions which could lead the team to new insights. The EMS Theological Orientation, Item 6, expresses this as follows: *We witness to the Gospel of Jesus Christ at all our respective places in an inviting and faithful way. The experience of being strangers to each other in encounters and in exchange across borders helps us to rediscover the Gospel in new ways.*

The following excerpts, taken from the much more extensive team visit reports, have been compiled by the editors of this book:

Team Visit I to the Presbyterian Church of Ghana (PCG), September 2015

Heike Bosien / Emmanuel Tettey / Riley Edwards-Raudonat

The Team Members' Understanding of Mission

"Mission is a great duty of all Christians. The goal of Mission is spiritual and holistic salvation. Mission needs unity and cooperation among all churches and organizations and various strategic approaches. To do mission is to show the Kingdom of God, especially in three areas: creation, celebration, peace." (Rev. Lee, Jung Gon, Presbyterian Church of Korea)

"For me, mission means that we as the church are sent by God to love our neighbours and let them know by words or deeds that they're loved by God. As I understand mission, it happens whenever

Christians are open for people outside their community." (Friederike Faller, Evangelical Church in Wuerttemberg)

"To me, mission is to reach out to different places and to different people, spreading and sharing the gospel." (Aphiwe Mpeka, Moravian Church in South Africa)

"I think you need a connection to the people and an exchange about faith to create an interest in Christian beliefs. If I know someone, I can talk with this person about my religion and my beliefs and give this person a chance to find his or her own beliefs. It is important for me to find together with the people the answers to their questions about religion." (Rahel Anne Römer, Evangelical Church in Baden)

"The high school I graduated from was founded by a missionary 25 years ago. Encountering Christianity there changed my life. Mission work need much time, much trouble, and a lot of people. It's not easy to find a suitable missionary approach. But Mysterious Hand will guide the missionaries certainly. For me, mission is educating people." (Asao Mochizuki, United Church of Christ, Japan)

"Mission for me means a common understanding of the global Christian community to stand together as one church with a calling to foster a just peace reconciliation among people, contribute to eco-justice and value and protect God's creation. Mission is bridge-building. The Minjung theology described it in that way: Go out of your own safeness." (Schulamit Kriener, German East Asia Mission, living in London)

"For me, mission means, making it possible for people to enjoy the fullness of life. Music is a very big part of mission. The music excites people. It makes people lively. For us in Ghana, music is a very big issue in mission work." (Emmanuel Tettey, Presbyterian Church of Ghana)

"We always see the Church as being in motion. It's a duty to go out and make disciples. The message must always go on." (Rev. Elizabeth Aduama, Presbyterian Church of Ghana)

"Mission today is an open process of listening to one another, sharing experiences from different churches and backgrounds in the world.

Mission today is a dialogue among brothers and sisters in the likeness of God." (Rev. Heike Bosien, Evangelical Church in Wuerttemberg)

Addressing the Questions – Discovering the Challenges of today

During our reflections at the end of the team visit we identified nine major issues, which should be further discussed in the EMS. These issues are the following:

a. *"The relationship between Gospel and Culture"*. In several places we have heard that we need an ongoing process to "Africanize Christianity". That still today the "Africanization of Christianity" is one of the challenges facing the PCG. The question, what this really looks like, produces a large variety of answers. The realization and implementation of this aim seems to be disparate.

b. *"Mission through Education"* – In a time when the government has been given extensive control over most PCG schools, the church finds itself asking how mission through education can best be retained.

c. *"Impact of Mission History on PCG today"*. It was amazing for us to realize how strong the reverence and adoration of the ancestors is in the Church in Ghana is. To what extent must the global mission history impact on the mission of the Church today?

d. *"Salvation in other religions?"* Through its Peace project and other forms of cooperation with Muslims, the PCG shows respect and tolerance towards Muslims in Ghanaian society. The theological question here is: is salvation as offered in the Islamic faith valid, even for Christians, or is Jesus Christ is the only way to God? How can the Church continue to engage in interfaith relations and dialogue without neglecting her mandate to evangelize and do mission?

e. *"Church and society in mutual relation"*. The PCG practices a "Mission to the palace" that means that the Church is involved in the lives of traditional leaders. What should be the terms of engagement between the Church and traditional leadership? How about 'mission to the state'? How can the Church engage the politician and get involved in political life as the voice of the voiceless?

f.   *"Pentecostalism, Charismatic and Apostolic Churches in competition"*: Inside and outside of the PCG there are charismatic initiatives on the one hand and traditional ways of worshipping on the other. How can the Churches bring these different strands of believers together?

g.   *"Mission Strategies in Ghana during the last two centuries"*: In the history of the PCG we see an important influence of the West Indies, of indigenous peoples, the use of mother tongue languages etc. In addition, the Basel Mission was never involved in the slave trade, meaning that its reputation is positive to this day. For the work today it is important to remain conscious of that learning process.

h.   *"The presence of the church in social service"*: Even today, the presence of the PCG in Diaconia, Education, Health and Social Services is immense. But how to deal with economic pressure in these areas? Wise behavior and prudent action is necessary.

i.   *"Reformation in the past and the meaning of Reformation today"*. Through the missionaries, the Reformation came to Ghana. "Our Luther is Zimmermann!" said Rev. Roger Wegurih. But what does Reformation mean today?

In the following part of this report we try to give answers to the list of questions of the EMS General Meeting in Arnoldshain November 2014:

1. How does the Presbyterian Church of Ghana understand mission in today's world? Does it have mission statements? If so: What topics do these statements address?

The Vision of the Presbyterian Church of Ghana is the following: We want *"To be a Christ Centered, Self-Sustaining and Growing Church."* Therefore in 2006 the church formulated a strategic plan for ten years. The content of this strategic plan is the statement titled "Our Mission". The mission statement of the Presbyterian Church of Ghana leads to the development of objectives and strategies to enable the Church to realize its vision. The focus of the PCG Mission is: "To uphold the centrality of the word of God and through the enablement of the Holy Spirit, pursue a holistic ministry so as to bring all of creation to glorify God." Concretely, the PCG wants to:

a. Mobilize the entire Church for Prayer.
b. Improve Church Growth through Evangelism and Nurture.
c. Attain self-sufficiency through effective resource mobilization.
d. Promote socio-economic development through advocacy and effective delivery of social services.
e. Uphold the reformed tradition.
f. Cherish partnership with the worldwide body of Christ.

We found the PCG Mission Statement as a poster every place where we met people. (…)

2. Who are the agents of mission in the PCG?

"There are no passengers on spaceship earth. We are all crew" (Marshall McLuhan). That means that every member of the church is an agent of mission. When the missionaries came to Ghana in 1828 they were seen as agents of God's Mission. But it was quickly clear that they could achieve nothing without the help of local people. "Culture and language [is something] you must know before converting people", said Rev. William Kwabena Ofosu Addo (Former National Director Missions and Evangelism for the PCG). "The role played by the indigenous people shouldn`t be missing", says Emmanuel Tettey. "We are always forgetting the black missionaries. For example Rev. Asante, the first ordained black minister", adds Elisabeth Aduama.

Tettey provides further detail: "The PCG has a strong force of lay people who support the ordained leaders in pursuing mission. The National Union of Presbyterian Students in Ghana (NUPSG) with its flagship program, the Presbyterian Students-In-Church Evangelism (P-SICE) plays a key role in evangelism. The general youth also have a similar evangelism program. Each congregation is supposed to have a group by name 'Bible Study and Prayer Group' (BSPG). The BSPG has part of its mandate to evangelize and plant new Churches. All the missionary work of the PCG is coordinated by the Department of Missions and Evangelism which is operational at all levels of the

Church. There is also the Department of Development and Social Services which sees to the rendering of social services in order to fulfil the holistic mission of the PCG. The ordained pastors and in some cases Catechists hold the ultimate responsibility as agents of mission for the PCG at the grassroots but much of the work is done by lay volunteer young and old members of the PCG."

3. What role does evangelization play and what forms of evangelization are deemed appropriate

As Chairperson Rev. Ansa-Peasa of Akyem Abuakwa Presbytery explains: "What we use for Evangelism is a peace-concept for the youth. That has to work through education and medicine…. When you try to evangelize you need something attractive to catch people. So we use music. When you sing people will definitively come! Today we are also using football to catch the youth. One hour of football, one hour of salvation message, and again one hour of football. It is very effective. We also use cinema for evangelism among the youth. Our plan in Akyem Abuakwa Presbytery is to have a full-time evangelism manager. 'To win one soul in your neighborhood' is one of our campaigns. It is coupled with welfare for church members and social work for non-church-members."

"The missionaries in the 19th century used street evangelism", says Rev. Asiama-Koranteng. "They sang to attract people. The missionaries started by singing simple songs." But they didn't stop there, Koranteng underlines. "They saw that the land was very fertile. So they introduced new farming methods and new crops: Cocoa, Cocoyam, Papayas. They distributed the fruits not only to those who were members of the Presbyterian Church." Agriculture became a mission method.

So these narratives tell of the method of evangelism used by the PCG. Different methods are used depending on the target community but what is mostly used is the 'house-to-house' or one-on-one evangelism, open air crusades.   These are generally accepted forms of evangelization in Ghana.

The PCG sees evangelism as a critical means to improve Church growth. (…) The holistic mission included the foundation of schools, the education of all people, the translation of the bible, health and agriculture.

4. How are other religions seen vis-à-vis such central themes as salvation or redemption?

The answer to that question depends on the person to whom you are talking. There are very close relations and also good cooperation with Muslims in different areas. For instance the peacemaking project and the activities of the Presbyterian Interfaith Research and Resource Centre through which Muslim women meet Christian women, Muslim youth meet Christian youth, and Muslim men meet Christian men. They discuss the vision of peace as a holistic concept for our daily lives.

Systematically and theologically spoken it is much more difficult to give an answer. In our meeting with PCG Moderator Rt. Rev. Prof. Emmanuel Martey we got the following answer: "The only eternal savior is Jesus. If you don't have the Spirit of Christ there is no salvation (Romans 8:9)." People of other religions "will enjoy 'bios' (the Greek word for 'life') but not eternal life." Yet salvation is not genetic. To become a Christian is not sufficient. You must join the born again movement."

Our question is this: If this position is consensus in the PCG, what about families in which the relatives belong to Christian and Islamic Faiths?

5. Turning now to the current 500th anniversary of the Reformation: In what way is the central protestant doctrine "justification by faith alone" a part of the PCG's mission understanding? What is the foundation of PCG's ethical teachings and how does this foundation relate to the core Reformation insight "by scripture alone"? To what extent does the PCG understand itself to be in a process of ongoing, continual Reformation?

The PCG has 'justification by faith alone' as one of her key doctrines which informs the teachings and content of her mission and evangelism activities.

The PCG also believes in the centrality of scripture (sola scriptura). As a way of always reminding her members of this belief, every chapel of the PCG has a large Bible lying open on the altar table. It affirms the centrality of the gospel, which in turn serves as the foundation for the ethical teachings of the PCG.

"The Reformation came to Ghana with the missionaries. The fact that they were not involved in the slavery trade gave them credibility compared to other missionaries. The Basel brought us the Bible. The Bible is as fresh as the newspaper this morning", says PCG Moderator Martey.

The proposition of a member of the team, Emmanuel Tettey appears to be an apt description of the PCG's disposition towards the Reformation. The concepts of the church cannot be static. The church needs a responsive setup, a constant, ongoing and continuous Reformation. We need to move people. We need to reform every day depending on the situation of every day.

"God`s word is powerful. Every church should be charismatic. If you do not believe in the gifts of the Holy Spirit you are not a church. Every church has to be Pentecostal, added PCG Moderator Martey.

6. Are diaconal or social components a part of the PCG mission concept? If so, what role do they play?

The PCG has as part of her mission statement, to 'pursue a holistic ministry so as to bring all of creation to glorify God' by 'promoting socio-economic development through advocacy and effective delivery of social services'. This is in continuity with the very beginnings of the church in 1828 until the present day 'Taking care of the people is a part of mission', says Elisabeth Aduama. It is closely connected. God has called us into the world for a purpose. (…)

The diaconal work of the PCG is planned and worked out by the Department of Development and Social Services which was set-up mainly for this purpose. The diaconal work of the PCG reflects in the areas of Agriculture, Health and Education. The PCG has hospitals, clinics and hundreds of school including primary schools, high schools, teacher training colleges and universities. In the past, the Church effectively used her schools as a means for mission, leading people to Christ and shaping the moral character of her students. But at the moment, the Church has little control over most of the schools since the government has assumed a controlling stake.

When we talk about social life we should not forget, the palace and the chiefs as an important aspect of Ghana's traditional political structure. The chief is thought to be a mediator between the ancestors and the living. The ancestors provide the living with all they need. Therefore the living have to bless them and to live with them in peace and harmony. The church with its social, medical, and educational work fulfils its role as Church looking for the Kingdom of God.

7. All of those involved in the team visits, be it the visitors or be it those being visited, are part and parcel of the "Evangelical Mission in Solidarity". What is the connection between "Mission" and "Solidarity" in the PCG? In what way is the connection being lived out in its ongoing work?

During our Visit the word "solidarity" didn't appear often in our conversations. It is a duty for the Church to be present for those who need help, for those who are poor, for those who are ill, for those who need education, for those who need comfort. It is the attitude of Jesus to be present for the marginalized and those in need. But the word "solidarity" is not the matrix of identification. "Mission" is the wording which is used in every conversation and for every area of church life and church work in the PCG. (...)

8. In the end: What is the overall effect of missionary endeavor as undertaken in and by the PCG?

Andreas Riis, who with others established the first mission station of the Basel Mission in Akropong, put it in this way: "The aim is not to make them Christians", but to give them the values of Christian living, "to give them moral standing." Emmanuel Tettey, some 165 years later, uses these words: The PCG is a growing Church with a holistic mission. Mission is holistic when head, hand and heart are touched by the mission of God. To do mission is to reach out to the head and the heart, the hands and the souls of the people." (…)

The increasing charismatic and Pentecostal movement means that a lot more has to be done to attract especially the youth to the PCG. False teachings by some pseudo-Christian groups and economic difficulties are all part of the difficulties that the PCG has to overcome. In facing these challenges, we recall the example of Fritz Ramseyer, one of the early Basel Missionaries to the then Gold Coast. Ramseyer was put in a forest and he had to battle the wild animals for his life. But Ramseyer triumphed with the use of just a bell to ward off the animals whenever they approached. So, the question now is what is the bell for the PCG and the worldwide Church today to overcome the challenges of mission? This is a question upon which the Church must continuously reflect order to maximise the missionary impact. God offers us creativity. Mission gives us the land to live this creativity offered by God.

Team Visit II to the Church of South India (CSI), October 2015

Riley Edwards-Raudonat

The Team Members on Mission, Before and After

Everyone interested in becoming a part of the Team was asked to submit a personal statement on the meaning of mission as a part of the application process. In the course of the visit, this original understanding was challenged by the various experiences the Team made. Accordingly, it was deemed appropriate to expand upon the original mission concepts once the trip had ended. Here a summary of that process, all persons speaking entirely for themselves.

- Rev. Lisjon Bagang (Basel Christian Church of Malaysia):
  Before: Mission is the core essence of the church. In my context, I was sent to my new ministry in 2014 as our church's agent of mission to our youth who are studying and working at West Malaysia.
  After: The central doctrine of the Reformation, namely "justification by faith alone", must remain at the centre of our missionary work.

- Jo Hanns Lehmann (Protestant Church in Hesse and Nassau):
  Before: Mission is for me to get to know each other, to learn from each other, to network, to help each other, to recognize the richness in diversity, to pray together and know that we are all one in Christ Jesus.
  After: I agree with the Moderator of the CSI: mission is bridge building.

- Rev. Riley Edwards-Raudonat (EMS Secretariat):
  Before: Mission is the communication of the Gospel of Jesus Christ. In the words of the late South African theologian David Bosch, this is best done in a spirit of "bold humility", remembering that actions always speak louder than words.
  After: The spirit of "bold humility" is complemented by the CSI's concept of "indirect mission", a strategy particularly suited to a

church living in a minority situation in a context in which mission is often equated with proselyting.

- Rev. Ebenezer Jathanna (Church of South India):
Before: Mission is meant for the entire human race, not for a particular people. Mission impacts and enhances the Christian values. Mission works from one generation to another. Mission moves on.
After: Mission is God's wonderful work and a great privilege in anyone's life. Mission work by itself has a very different perspective. If we see what Mission work is really all about, we will be enriched by the experience and be influenced by it. Mission is a like a seed. It has the strength to produce lots of fruit and lots of seed.

- Christiane Rößler   (Protestant Church of the Palatinate):
Before: Mission to me is the transmission of our Christian faith. As I am a deaconess, word and deed are inseparable to me. As I understand it, mission always comprises two sides: an interior as well as an exterior one. If we live our lives true to both, then both sides can profit from each other.
After: Mission allows us to sense something of the Kingdom of God, which begins here on earth and transcends distance as well as political and cultural borders. Sharing our faith is a deeply positive experience. The task, grounded in our faith, is to assume social responsibility, remaining sensitive to the respective religious-cultural context as we do so. In this, we support each other as the situation permits.

- Rev. Ralf Rohrbach-Koop (Basel Mission German Branch):
Before: Missio dei! God sets us into motion for his mission.
After: Missio Dei! God's ways in moving us, sharing and living out his gospel are so manifold ways that I am astonished and challenged. Missio Dei means to be open and surprised how God will work even through me. Sometimes it doesn't even need any deep reflections or planning. It's just being there as an authentic Christian in our so differing multicultural situations. Christ's incarnation can happen anywhere, but it's challenging and changing everywhere. And India – of course – has been widening my horizon!

- Ni Made Rai Margharita Sunami (Christian Protestant Church in Bali): *Before*: Mission is about fulfilling the Great Commission based on God's love for the world. It means having the passion to do everything with the purpose of glorifying the Name of the Lord Jesus Christ. It means sharing the good news of God's free gift of salvation in a personal, loving and peaceful approach without offending the religion or beliefs of others at any time, anywhere at any cost.
  After: Mission in the context of the CSI is an indirect way of outreaching; introducing Christian values to the community through all kinds of humanitarian activities as needed for such pluralistic society with various religions as in India.

- Rev. Dr. Royce Victor (EMS India Liaison officer, CSI):
  Before: Mission is joyful journeying with God to share the love of God with all creations, and to be with the broken communities in their struggle to face the challenges of life.
  After: Mission moves through people of all generations in all directions. We are called to partake in God's mission in our own time and space.

Addressing the Questions: The Team at Work

1. How does the Church in South India (CSI) understand mission in today's world? Does it have mission statements? If so: What topics do these statements address?

It was no trouble for the Team to find the CSI Mission Statement. Upon arrival in Chennai, the Team proceeded to the CSI Synod Offices and Guest House, where it found the CSI Mission Statement posted in several places throughout the building. As a delegation of the Evangelical Mission in Solidarity, the Team couldn't help but be pleased with a mission statement expressing the Church's "solidarity with the broken communities". In the course of our visit, the Team saw several examples of this concern. These are described in more detail below under question five: "Diaconal and social components". The coupling of the mission statement with five "mission priorities" for the years 2011-2020 was perceived as a useful and effective way of insuring that the mission statement is indeed implemented and that this implementation is monitored.

However, this statement of the CSI as a whole was not the only mission statement encountered. At least one church institution, namely the Hebich Technical Institute in Mangalore, has formulated a Vision and Mission Statement of its own, which is proudly posted at the institution's entrance (see left). Here, however, the word "mission" is being used in a slightly different sense, its frame of reference being the goal of a solid technical education rather than the communication of the gospel. Or can it be said that this goal is rather a concrete expression of the gospel?

2. Who are the agents of mission in the CSI?

This question was a recurring one throughout the Team Visit. As the Visit took place during the 200th Anniversary Celebrations of the Basel Mission, it was only natural that much attention was given to the first agents of mission in India, namely the missionaries whose ground-breaking work in the 19th century laid an important cornerstone for the CSI of today. Several of the presentations given during the International Mission Seminar dealt with their work, their achievements and their shortcomings. One aspect our group found particularly interesting was developed by CSI General Secretary Rev. Dr. D.R. Sadananda in his keynote address "From Mission Compounds to a Borderless Church" at the International Seminar.

As Sadananda explained, the Basel Missionaries were never the sole agents of mission, even in the 19th century. Many Indians were involved as well. One example used was that of persons of Shudra origin, who after becoming Christian sometimes gained employment as teachers in the Basel Mission schools. There, it could well transpire that such teachers would find themselves instructing students originally from upper caste background. As Sadananda observed, this was a clear example of "mission from the margins" long before the World Council of Churches called for such activity in its position paper "Together towards Life" in 2013.

At this juncture, the Team would also like to note that from all appearances, there are only a very few women serving as pastors or in leadership positions in the CSI, the female Bishop Rt. Rev. Pushpa Lalitha being a notable exception. The Team was privileged to meet with Rev. Sharath Sowseelya, who described her role as a female pastor at length. On the whole, her presentation was positive. There was no doubt that she is happy to be a CSI pastor. At the same time, she made clear that she often experiences subtle forms of discrimination. Bridal couples sometimes avoid her, turning to male colleagues to perform their Blessing Ceremonies. Male pastoral colleagues sometimes make demeaning remarks. Beyond this, the Team met women serving as leaders only in schools or in children's homes.

3. What role does evangelization play and what forms of evangelization are deemed appropriate?

In a very gracious setting, namely an evening meal on Tuesday, Oct. 5 at the home of Karnataka Theological Seminary Principal Rev. Dr. Honeybal Cabral with many invited guests, the Team was given the opportunity to ask questions. A Team member was quick to respond: "What is the current position of the CSI on evangelism?" Though it was not the intention, the Team had the impression that with this question, it had put its hosts on the defensive. Perhaps it would have been better to have phrased the question as it is listed above. At any rate, a very interesting discussion on evangelism ensued.

The initial response came from Dr. Cabral himself: "The old tradition of freely exchanging views in the marketplace is no longer the practice. Nowadays in India, we use an 'indirect approach.'" As the Team was not familiar with this term, it had to be explained. As the Team came to understood it, "indirect mission" is the silent witness of good deeds performed by Christians to and for the wider community. Evangelism is therefore now more a matter of faith formation, living the Christian life in such a way that it makes a positive impression on an outsider. As one person continued: "We know that there is a reluctance to convert. It may result in a loss of status in family life. Accordingly, we accept that persons may be sympathetic to the

Christian cause, yet hesitate to leave their own religious background and take on a new religious identity." Others went on to explain that in modern India, secularism is seen as strength, as it enables persons of various religious persuasions to live together peacefully. (…)

4. How are other religions seen vis-à-vis such central themes as salvation or redemption?

Certainly, the Team observed that within the CSI, traditional understandings of salvation or redemption remain in place. This was evident in the liturgy used in the communion celebration during the Inaugural Thanksgiving Service for the formation of the new CSI Malabar Diocese on Sunday, Oct. 11: "Lord, we your servants do this in remembrance of him as he commanded, until his coming again, giving thanks to you for the perfect redemption (italics added) which you have brought about for us in him."

However, it seemed to us that there is a certain reluctance to take up such topics with reference to other religions. At one point, for example, the Team were advised by its Indian hosts that such topics could be difficult, bringing about tension. Certainly, at no time during our visit was anyone heard passing judgment on understandings of salvation or redemption in Hinduism, Buddhism or Islam, to name only the three most prominent non-Christian religions in India. The Team also refrained from any kind of value statement. Nonetheless, the Team was left with an open question: Is dialogue on such topics possible? Is there a context in which it is being conducted? In the estimation of the Team, this is something that could be further explored.

5. Turning now to the current 500th anniversary of the Reformation: In what way is the central protestant doctrine "justification by faith alone" a part of the CSI's mission understanding? What is the foundation of CSI's ethical teachings and how does this foundation relate to the core Reformation insight "by scripture alone"? To what extent does the CSI understand itself to be in a process of ongoing, continual Reformation?

It was only one occasion during the visit that the topic "Reformation Theology" was explicitly treated. This was at a Pastors' Conference which took place in the Karkala Bethania Church on Oct. 6. Here again, the Team was first introduced and then given the opportunity to ask the group a question or two. The question asked was "Does the central Reformation doctrine 'Justification by Faith' still play a role in the life and faith of the church in India today?" But the answers were directed to a different question, namely that of "Justification by Christian Faith". This led to several responses on the part of those present on the necessity of respecting other religions. The general tone of these responses was that the CSI strives for "unity in diversity".

It is, of course, simply not possible to take this one encounter as representative for the CSI as a whole. Our question was unexpected; no one had a chance to prepare for it in advance. In the opinion of the Team, the question had been misunderstood, and time did not permit its being phrased anew. All the same, the encounter was significant. Persons present who happened to meet the group later on took up the topic again. One such person, Rev. Edwin Joseph, remarked the following day that in his opinion, a "new Reformation" is needed, this one addressing the religious yearnings of persons now leaving the church in search of other types of spirituality. It also remained a topic for the Team. In the closing evaluation, one Team Member remarked that "I'm still thinking about the justification issue. To me, justification by faith is at the core of Christian faith in the Protestant tradition. I don't understand the CSI position on this point." Another added that "though we asked what Reformation theology means today, we didn't talk about it." This person went on to say that "more theological dialogue is necessary.", Of course, there may well be more theological dialogue taking place than the Team was exposed to during its brief visit.

6. Are diaconal or social components a part of the CSI mission concept? If so, what role do they play?

As mentioned above, the mission understanding of the CSI as the Team came to understand is in its entire essence diaconal. This was more than evident during the International Seminar, which over and again made reference to the holistic approach employed by the Basel Mission in the 19th century. The tile factories, the mission schools, the medical mission – all this and more laid the groundwork for the diaconal understanding of mission in the modern-day CSI.

The Team was introduced to the current diaconal activities of the CSI by Rev. Asir Ebenezer, CSI Director for Diaconal Concerns. He indicated that the following communities make up the focus of these efforts:

- Dalit and Tribal Communities
- Women – including Concerns Relating to Human Trafficking
- Children – particularly children at risk and the female child
- Migrant labourers
- Sexual and gender minorities
- Small, marginal and tenant farmers
- Landless agricultural labourers
- Persons living with and affected by HIV / AIDS
- Persons with disabilities
- Rural households inaccessible to quality affordable health care
- Unemployed youth
- Seafarers

(…) Of particular interest to the group was the item "Sexual and Gender Minorities". In conversation with Ebenezer, the Team learned that this refers largely to transgender persons. This phenomenon, long present in India, is mentioned in the Bible (eunuchs) and has apparently gained some acceptance in the CSI. As the Team understood it, there is now a CSI pastor who is of transgender orientation, indicating increasing acceptance. Persons of gay / lesbian orientation, however, apparently have a different status. In particular, there is disagreement within the church as to their suitability for ordination to the pastoral ministry.

A central aspect of diaconal in the CSI is its concern for the Dalit, a highly-marginalized group in Indian society. One very interesting approach towards inclusion and uplifting of the Dalit is the newly-published coffee table book "Dalit Brush", produced by the CSI with the assistance of both the Evangelical Mission in Solidarity (EMS) and the Association of Churches and Missions in Germany (EMW). The art work is done by Dalits and is therefore often autobiographical, depicting the struggles of the artists themselves. (…)

7. All of those involved in the team visits, be it the visitors or be it those being visited, are part and parcel of the "Evangelical Mission in Solidarity". What is the connection between "Mission" and "Solidarity" in the CSI? In what way is the connection being lived out in its ongoing work?

Here, it should be fair to say that the impressions of the group were conflicting. On the one hand, the Team could not help but be impressed by the many concrete examples of solidarity being shown to various marginalized groups in Indian society. Several of these have been itemized immediately above.

On the other hand, however, there were moments in the course of the trip which surprised the Team. It were pleased, for example, to visit the old tile factory in Mangalore, once founded by the Basel Mission, and to realize that it is still in operation today, though it is now owned and operated privately. However, the Team could not help but notice that those working in the factory now are migrants from other parts of India, and that much of the machinery being used was quite old, which of course increases the risk of injury.

The Team also had a look at some of the housing the workers use, and found it a strange juxtaposition that these meagre quarters were overshadowed by a large and expensive house higher up on the hill. Certainly: Pictures like this can be taken the world over. No society is free of poverty. Still, this scene remains with the group as an indication that much remains to be done in the name of solidarity, in India, and in the rest of the world as well! However, let us not forget that the CSI has included the Church's "solidarity with the broken communities" as part of its Mission Statement (see above). In other words: Solidarity is very much on the CSI agenda.

8. In the end: What is the overall effect of missionary endeavour as undertaken in and by the CSI?

To be honest: There is really no way for the Team Visit, after a stay of some ten days, to assess the overall effect of mission past and present in the CSI. Let us rather include here a few general observations, with no attempt to answer the question in its entirety.

- It was particularly interesting to the Team that during the International Seminar, several of those presenting were non-Christians. Their very presence indicated a strong recognition of the missionary efforts in the 19th century by the society as a whole. Certainly, these persons were sometimes critical. They mentioned that the missionaries were sometimes too quick to be judgmental, as for example when they would asses a person to be a "half convert" or a "full convert". (…) Still: The overall assessment was positive. More than enough evidence was given that the missionary efforts of the 19th century benefited India as a whole, both its Christian and its non-Christian populations.
- Over and again, reference was made to the "3000 missionaries" currently doing evangelistic work in the CSI, largely in a rural setting. It seemed to the Team that this is truly mission "to the marginalized", so that it would have liked to have seen some of the work they are doing first-hand. Still, the Team was encouraged by the fact that in spite of the difficulties involved, the CSI still wishes to be active in missionary outreach, searching as it does so for methods appropriate to the situation at hand.
- The Team could not help but be impressed by the CSI's enormous organizational abilities. Everywhere the Team was taken, its reception had been carefully prepared. The worship services were colourful, augmented by a wide range of choral performances and extremely well-attended by both young and old. The International Seminar in commemoration of the Basel Mission Bicentenary had obviously been gaining momentum for months, suddenly exploding onto the scene with its beginning on Oct. 8 and giving all involved food for thought for years to come. (…) As we turn now to the next century of mission, the "Mission Moves Team" can only hope that the CSI with its wealth of experience and enormous drive will be at the forefront.

Team Visit III to the Protestant Indonesian Church in Donggala (GPID), April 2016

Kerstin Neumann

The Team Members on Mission, Before and After

Before

Everyone interested in joining the Team was asked to submit a personal statement on the meaning of mission as a part of the application process. Here you find those original statements, all persons speaking entirely for themselves.

- Wayan Ardiawan (GPID General Secretary): Mission to me includes all aspects of life and ministry, both physical and spiritual needs, which we endeavor to serve through Holistic Mission covering Koinonia (Sunday congregational services and weekday services for smaller groups within the church), Marturia (preaching and evangelism) and Diakonia (ministry to the needy within the church). Mission is not just introducing God's word to others or bringing people to become Christians, but how the Good News is reflected in the life of each person.
- Reinhard Brand (Evangelical Church of Kurhessen-Waldeck): Mission of the church means to participate in God's movement towards the world to proclaim the Gospel and to support its realization (Luke 3:18-19). [Needed are] experiences in programs to make the Gospel relevant / meaningful for people in secular contexts.
- Minju Cho (Presbyterian Church of Korea): I do not think that the concept of mission is just building and forming a religious church in foreign countries. I am more concerned about the faith community based on its own tradition and original culture, whether local or global. It is not right, I think, that the mission should only be concerned about religions, especially Christianity. It has to be considered with respect to peoples, traditions and cultures.

- Ilka Friedrich (Protestant Church in Hesse and Nassau): Jesus himself asks in Mark 10:36: "What is it you want me to do for you?" This verse gets to the heart of my understanding of mission. In following the path of Jesus, we have the mission to evangelize by listening, talking and doing the gospel. Mission is to bring and to learn the message of love and salvation which God offers his creation (…). It is a big challenge to work for peace and justice in the world together with others – as an identifiable Christian – and to learn from each other.

- Ebnezar Jathanna (Church of South India): Mission is transformation. Mission is to transform people towards God.

- William Lo (Basel Christian Church of Malaysia): Mission is a centre of church life and church growth because it is God's Great Commission to us.

- Kai Tobias Lüke (German East Asia Mission): Mission means bridging spiritual needs and orientation towards social issues, to overcome the separation of Christians and practice unity as children of God.

- Kerstin Neumann (EMS Secretariat): To my mind, mission is a way of being. It is our faithful response, through which we tune into God´s transformative work and weave in God's creation, of which we are part.

- Dewiartati Sorongan (GPID): A mission statement is a way of communicating the purpose of an organization. It should guide the action of the organization, spell out its overall goals, provide a path and guide decision-making. It provides "the frame or context within which the organization's strategies are formulated". It is like a goal for what we want to do for the world.

After

In the course of the visit, these original understandings were challenged by the various experiences the Team made. Accordingly, it was deemed appropriate to expand upon the original mission concepts once the trip had ended. Kai Lüke formulated the following text, which was adopted by the Team at the close of the visit:

"The Slogan 'Mission Moves' applies not only for the 200th Anniversary of the Basel Mission, but also for the Reformation

Commemoration and for the EMS Fellowship at the very core of its existence. There are mission movements in the traditional sense, then and now, from Europe into the wider world and now back from the wider world to Europe. Then there is the fact that mission moves us in the much broader sense of the word ´mission´: as people of God, we are moved from within, touched by the sense of unity in all we have in common and, at the same time, enriched by all the differences that supposedly separate us. These differences can serve to open our eyes, so that we see and experience our faith anew, over and again, from other perspectives. We may thus not only accept but also respect and appreciate differences. Wherever we gain the impression that we cannot live with an attitude different from our own, we should feel challenged to question and re-work our own position.

Mission means to work for God on earth towards a better world, here and now. However, humans are never perfect and therefore the church is in need of constant reformation. Mission moves us and pushes us today – just as in the days of Martin Luther and Jan Hus - to never accept a status quo.

Our reflections in the course of the Team Visit further led us to a new mode of encounter with others. Realizing that mission is a sensitive topic, we as a Team learned to take more time to listen rather than to quickly pass judgment, and we learned to focus on what we have in common without giving up personal convictions. To use the familiar expression coined by William Lo: "Maybe I am wrong, correct me, but…"

Addressing the Questions: The Team at Work

1. How does the Protestant Indonesian Church in Donggala (GPID) understand mission in today's world? Does it have mission statements? If so: What topics do these statements address?

> *"To create a community of believers who are obedient, faithful, and fear the Lord God, Maker of the universe, and to be responsible for building a society and nation that is united, peaceful, prosperous, and true to the testimony of the Bible."*

This confession, Tujuan GPID, was translated for the EMS Team during our first meeting with the leadership of the church from Bahasa Indonesian as 'the aim of the church'. The image used by the office bearers to describe their self-understanding was that of the potter and the clay indicating their readiness to allow God to mould his people and his church.

To learn what mission means in Central Sulawesi requires a lot of travelling. The Team enjoyed it from the beginning, not only because of the beautiful landscapes but also because of the opportunities to talk, the time to ask questions and the chances to share opinions.

The GPID at its founding consisted of 48 congregations. In 1937, it grew out of the Dutch East India Church as part of the GMIM, forming the GPID as an independent church in April 1965 outside the confines of GMIM. The start was made with 8 pastors and 3 evangelists; today there are 173 congregations and 20 outreach posts served by 109 pastors. There are about 8.550 families in 48 congregations with more than 60% of them in remote areas. But reaching out to people is not only a question of covering distances, there are 33 ethnic groups within GPID that speak more than a hundred languages.

During the celebration of the church's 51st birthday with a seminar for all GPID pastors in Walandano we learn more: Mission is praxis, is helping to improve living conditions and thus the quality of life by rendering health services and by offering educational support. It is the continuous attempt to shape a community by instilling Christian values and to hold it together in spite of diverse cultural identities and language barriers. This is done in the face of the often sensitive task of living with the Muslim majority and in view of formidable challenges such as environmental degradation and the threat of terrorism.

Isn't it striking that the mission statement speaks of building the society and the nation? In particular, the diaconal work of the church serves to sustain communities: health care and education for all.

Over and again, we were left speechless while learning about and experiencing in detail the GPID's mission tasks. The determination with which these tasks are undertaken and the joy that accompanies the work were overwhelming and held in high esteem by the Team throughout our stay.

The organization of the Pastors' Conference in Walandano is itself an example: a rather small congregation spends roughly a year preparing for some 60 to 70 participants, the biggest challenge being the supply of sweet water for all. During the church's anniversary service, the EMS Team expressed a word of thanks and a greeting, then sang two songs, one in Bahasa Indonesia, and was accepted and ´assimilated´ into the celebrating community as if we had been friends for a very long time.

2. Who are the agents of mission in the GPID?

It is in relation to the question "Who are the agents of mission?" that we had the most intense and at times controversial debates.

Agents are the church leaders of course, and the pastors who serve in congregations sharing the Gospel and supporting communities according to their needs.

Internally there is an organization of GPID churches in columns. Kai Lüke compared them to a system he is familiar with in the Moravian community: columns make sure that all members are in touch with the church with the help of rotating house prayers and visits.

Information gained in the church services we attended as well as in the discussions with pastors during the Church Anniversary in Walandano left no doubt as to the crucial role of the church's elders. They often hold important and responsible positions in the society. Their handling of the church's money makes them powerful players within the church as well.

During our trip, we visited the local GPID Seminary "Marturia" in Palu, Marturia. It is financed in part with the help of a Kindergarten that is located on the premises. All students present expressed their concern about the importance of theological education not only for pastors, but also for Sunday school teachers and school trainers, all of them being agents of mission. Many students study as private candidates, without endorsement of the church. Since they have to finance their studies on their own, they sometimes come for a term or two and then "disappear" in order to earn money. Since in addition to the fees the cost of accommodation and board must also be managed, the financial burden is impossible to bear for most students in Marturia. (…)

Regarding theological education it is also of importance to consider that college education is not enough, as it doesn't equip a person for pastoral work. She or he must be accustomed to the language and the culture of the congregation where s/he is to work: a fishing community needs a pastor familiar with their concerns, a farming group needs a farmer, etc. Five years of college education plus 2-3 years as assistant of a pastor add up to a job that does not pay more than 260 USD per month, at least during the first years of service.

We found it interesting in this connection to see that more than 50% of the pastors are female whereas among the elders they hold only 5% of the posts. The question of women leadership in our churches of different contexts became a topic of continuing debate. We all appreciated GPID General Secretary Zakharias Widodo's wish for a woman to succeed him. However, the church has to be prepared for a woman leader and the women for leadership would have to participate in capacity building measures in order to be empowered for such a task.

Women sustain the church work and are therefore most important agents of mission in the GPID. During a sharing session with the Women's Commission, we were impressed by the wide range of activities women engage in. They are active the areas of Koinonia, Mission of the Gospel, Diakonia and Administration. In practical terms, this includes the organization of the Women's Day, outreach programs for spiritual refreshment with an emphasis on disadvantaged women, assisting with an orphanage and a pre-school and participation in the Asian Church Women's Conference, among others. (…)

3. What role does evangelization play and what forms of evangelization are deemed appropriate?

Sumbersari is habituated by immigrant Christians from Bali. Their cultural expression of being Christian is very much shaped by the Hindu context in which they lived before settling in the coastal region of central Western Sulawesi. We feel the difference in culture in the church we visit. To most of us it appears like a Hindu temple rather than a Christian church.

Pastors and elders come well prepared to the afternoon meeting, sharing cake, tea and juice in the church. "We tell the good news to the people. It is up to God to work in their lives. Mission is accomplished through the various church activities and outreach programs for people irrespective of faith: harmonious interfaith relations are important," one of the elders argues, himself head of education in Sumbersari. The Team sensed an interesting contrast between the focus on the very specific characteristics of the Balinese migrant culture in Sumbersari on the one hand and an understanding of mission and evangelization that frequently uses the term 'to bring' on the other. The indication is that one cannot move exclusively within one's own church confines, but must bring the Gospel to others. (…)

"All we do in life is dependent on our religion." This statement of a female pastor is reflected in the comprehensive understanding of evangelization in the Indonesian context. Evangelization means building churches to win people and offer them a space that gives meaning to their lives. In Sumbersari this means making use of the cultural riches brought from Bali. They are a God-given gift, shared by Hindus and Christians of the region, contextualized into the theology and rituals of the 33 congregations belonging to the Bali migrant community. In a comprehensive discussion on the role of culture and inculturation we learn that the community identity of the Balinese Christians in the area is very strong. Culture is understood to be part of the 'holistic mission' of the church. Holistic does not leave cultural characteristics aside but uses them for an active and creative formulation of who the Christians in Sumbersari are. Their traditional Gamelan music, for example, plays an important role. So does classical dance, performed in school competitions. Hindus of the region do the same and are often doing better. The same applies to their decorative art work which beautifies the church premises.

Our understanding of mission and evangelization as being shaped by the cultural and social context in which we grew up accompanies the Team throughout. Among ourselves we continually discuss: Evangelization is not simply about converting people to the Christian faith. It is also not a question of preaching alone but of living and sharing the

Good News. We all agree. The Western perspective insists on critically questioning and analyzing the attitude of the missionaries during their missionary activities. The Asian side emphasizes the need to fellowship for all church members, the newly-converted as well as the well-established ones. What is required to be a Christian? How does one become a good Christian? For Rev. Ardiawan, it is clear: "You must have fellowship." The primary task of a minister is to keep the congregation together. If a family doesn't come to church for a month the pastor will surely go to inquire. The German reaction: If a pastor goes to a person or family who has not attended church services for four weeks to find out the cause for such behaviour, the person in question might leave the church for good.

Throughout the day in the church of Sumbersari it was the huge wooden cross that kept reminding us of differences we may not be able to set aside. All around it were small red, green and blue lights that continually flickered. Disturbed by the lighting effects fixed to a symbol that stands for Jesus' suffering, Ilka Friedrich asked about its meaning. It is not Bali culture, we are told, rather modern culture. "For our sense of aesthetics, the lights make the cross pretty: it has to shine!"

4. How are other religions seen vis-à-vis such central themes as salvation or redemption?

Talking about other religions in Indonesia means talking first and foremost about Islam. Half way through our Team Visit program, and having experienced the omnipresence of the Islamic religion, we have a meeting with the Islamic organization Alkhairaat. It is a high profile encounter, to which the GPID, the PGI as well as Alkhairaat send their leadership. Immediately prior to the arrival of Alkhairaat General Secretary Dr Lukman with his team, EMS Team member Ebnezar Jathanna elects to change the seating arrangement. We are grateful to sit in a circle rather than in rows, now facing one another while talking.

In an atmosphere of respect, openness and mutual interest we are informed by the Muslim group that the night before our meeting, an Islamic school in one of the North Molukku islands had been burnt, the perpetrators most likely being Christian. This and other delicate issues are put forth, and we are well-aware that this is possible only on the basis of goodwill and trust in each other and the shared conviction that good relationships, irrespective of religion, are crucial in avoiding extremes. All agree that the increasing influence of Islamic missionaries of Wahhabi background is to be feared and countered in friendship. There is unrest in Central Sulawesi, particularly in the region south of Palu, ever since the 1950's. The Christians are of the opinion that the traditionally good relations between Muslims and Christians are becoming cooler due to the fear of terrorism. The Indonesian Government is trying to get rid of Islamic militants who seem to have a training camp in the Poso region south of Palu. People have reason to be afraid; some do not even dare to go to church on Sundays. A coffee plantation near Walandano, started with the help of EMS, cannot be cared for now; nobody would dare to raise crops in this part of the island. (…)

When talking about national identity in Indonesia, reference is made to the Pancasila, the five principles upon which the Indonesian nation rests: nationalism, humanism, social justice for all, unity and – usually in a prominent place – the oneness of the divine. The term Tuhan for "Lord" guarantees that each citizen can feel included.

A lot should be said and still much more researched and discovered about the indigenous religious traditions of the many Indonesian islands.

5. Turning now to the current 500th anniversary of the Reformation: To what extent does the GPID understand itself to be in a process of ongoing, continual Reformation?

Talking about the future means talking about youth. The first and foremost information we received on youth is that huge numbers of them migrate upon completing high school. They do not see a future in the rural areas and prefer of feel forced to go to cities to find jobs or places of higher education. These young people attend church services in the city congregations, but many are attracted to evangelical or Pentecostal churches where they find the music to be more to their liking than that of the traditional church services. Many GPID adults are alarmed that so many young people are no longer interested in attending church services, considering the hymns to be too old-fashioned. They prefer to organize their own services, in which they can perform and sing in their own style of music, i.e. making use of popular and current Indonesian songs.

Our talk with the GPID youth leaders starts with a long warm-up, organized as our last event before leaving Palu to return home. Maybe it would have been an easier sharing among peers only.

Topics and issues the youth deals with - depending of course on where they come from:

- The challenge of the technological explosion
- Drugs – cooperation of different departments needed
- HIV/AIDS – requires training and moral teaching
- Commitment to the church, unifying youth

Duties of the youth groups and their leaders:

- Community support: Distributing food to the needy
- Raising money for outreach programs through painting and cleaning projects
- Visiting Youth groups of other congregations
- Taking care of a congregation of newly-converted persons
- Taking up special assignments by elders
- Youth services on Saturday evenings using popular Indonesian music!

Topics that were mentioned but proved difficult to discuss included drugs and 'liberal attitudes' towards sex. We were told that drugs are a growing problem in the Indonesian society, good cooperation with Government agencies being is considered to be crucial. All were aware that HIV/AIDS is an issue that would require good information and training programs, or rather 'moral' teaching, as some said. The established congregations try to instil in the youth concern for diaconal work and the importance of obtaining community support. Talking about human sexuality is very difficult, if not impossible. "You can't go into detail, just remain within the broader picture", is a frequent answer.

The challenges the youth face are complex and of course depend on the social and family background. One serious challenge is technological explosion. In the cities many youth are deeply involved in lifestyles that make church life appear superfluous. Attendance and a vivid interest in church affairs is found to be more prevalent among the rural youth. The biggest challenge for young persons in the GPID is to insure that they don't lose their commitment. (…)

For the GPID, 'Reformasi' is an essential part of the confession that focuses on sola gratia, sola fide, sola scriptura and, at the core, solo Christo. As GPID General Secretary Zakharias Widodo emphasizes, the Heidelberg Catechism is a shared document. The theologies of Luther and Calvin determine the theological outlook of the church. Today, the church is engaged in the concern for peace and justice because this is the most pressing issue. In a comprehensive paper on what reformation means to his church, Widodo summarizes: "Mission is all efforts to proclaim Euangelion (Good News) universally and holistically, to proclaim freedom to the poor, to the blind, to the people who are under pressure and persecuted because of their faith, to proclaim that the Year of the Lord's Grace has come!"

6. Are diaconal or social components a part of the GPID mission concept? If so, what role do they play?

This issue was discussed in a most practical way during the group discussions with the pastors in Walandano. Out of their daily routine and in good spirits, they welcomed the opportunity to share concerns and difficulties. Many of them opened up and gave the visiting Team deep insights into diaconal aspects of the GPID's mission work. First and foremost, family counselling was mentioned. The pastors appreciate the spiritual strength of their people. They attend the services and programs the church offers. Even if they are migrants in the sense that they have found a job in a nearby factory, they participate as long as the employment in the area lasts.

In the more remote regions, economic problems are a fact of daily life. Many church members work in palm oil plantations or gold mines; others go to the cities to find employment. The rural churches, however, will not be closing. 'Local people' have lots of children, is an explanation expressed with laughter.

However, the divorce rate seems to be on the increase. There are men who just move away, find another job in another place and find another wife as well, leaving it to the women left behind to take care of the children on their own.

The GPID engages in poverty eradication as well as in empowerment programs. In Sumbersari, for example, we are introduced to a Micro Credit program supported financially by a Dutch organization but administered by the Synod office. Anyone can become a member of the credit society irrespective of religious affiliation. Only members can apply for loans. The church is quite proud of this organization. There are now four offices in Sulawesi alone, one of them being in Luwu. This is a great extension and an expression of the people's longing to accept support to improve their living conditions. The micro or small-scale loans are given for projects in the areas of industry, commercial ventures and farming. Among these, only those in agriculture are financed with longer periods of repayment. Interestingly, borrowing money is possible only if the borrower agrees to save money as well. Members receive a good interest rate of about 12%, and it is only about one in a hundred persons who finds it difficult to repay. Of further interest is the fact that women are preferred as loan holders for the simple fact that they are more reliable than men.

The baseline of diaconal and social components as integral part of the GPID mission concept is convincingly repeated in our encounters and discussions with GPID members of all walks of life. The church has a vivid interest in community development beyond the Christian church, irrespective of the religious affiliation of those involved. For the region, this is seen as crucial. It is the best way to assure safety and to enable the church to prosper.

(...) During the evening reflection the Team expressed how thoroughly it was impressed by this request for the church to take such an active role in shaping the social life of the Sulawesi society.

7. What is the connection between "Mission" and "Solidarity" in GPID? In what way is this connection being lived out in its ongoing work?

The combination of mission and solidarity was most convincingly presented by the young vicar Rev. Aldi in the village Ongulara-Pompa. However, his approach is not singular to him alone. It is typical of the commitment to their work shown by many pastors and church leaders. The church building in Ongulara-Pompa was constructed at the time of the foundation of the congregation in the year 2004. We met the entire village there; a children's choir received us with songs. We ate violet-colored sweet potatoes and engaged in the sharing of life concerns with the help of two interpreters: one translating from English to Bahasa Indonesia, the other from Bahasa Indonesia to Da'a, one of the sixteen languages of the area.

We learned that a community like the one in Ongulara-Pompa are referred to as the "unreached." Oh yes, they are certainly difficult to reach in terms of getting to their villages. We know, having travelled by car, by raft and on motorbike in order to "reach" them.

But who are the "unreached," the Team later discussed: Isn't God already there, long before a church is built? Is it our perspective that sets the standard for being reached, our form of spirituality that determines what Christian faith is?

Vicar Aldi calls them 'young in faith' – an expression we should elaborate further. We speak of 53 families with 175 members. We know little about the content of their faith or how strong it is. Church to them is a social institution and their belief is surely strongly characterized by this sense of belonging together. Everything they say about God must to be seen from the perspective of their traditional beliefs. It must further be said that in all likelihood, our question about God per se didn't make much sense to them. Most important to them are the festivals of life, harvest and birth in particular, both incorporating traditional elements.

In a later inner-Team discussion, Paul as depicted in Acts came into play, believing in the unknown god. What are the indicators of changing faith? Baptism alone? Can we come up with criteria? What makes a Christian a Christian?

All enjoy singing most, so that this seems to be an important part of coming to church. The children sang with great commitment.

We found the church building to be rudimentary indeed, a reflection of the material poverty of the congregation itself. What do its members wish for their families? "Education for the children and health care for all." What makes them sad? "When there is not enough to eat or when someone is sick." What is all theological reason when compared to the wisdom of the villagers: "You have come from very far to meet and talk to us. This would not have been possible without God."

We were all impressed by Vicar Aldi´s work. We came to know him as being one with the community, not easy to make out in the group and without his being introduced as the pastor in charge. (…)

8. In the end: What is the overall effect of missionary endeavour as undertaken in and by the GPID?

As GPID General Secretary Zakharias Widodo himself as written: "The overall effect of missionary endeavor as undertaken in and by the GPID, especially in the 50th year of its Synod, is as follows: GPID has become self-supporting in mission, increased the number of its churches, pastors, presbyters, deacons and vicars, gained new Christians especially from original tribes, operates a training center, a plantation/farm, schools from elementary level to that of a theological seminary, an orphanage, maintains good relations with the Government and different non-governmental organizations such as inter-religious and inter-denominational groups on the local, regional, national and global levels. We have a new Synod Office in Kijang Street, Palu, have good programs, projects and human resources to empower people, have the GPID Confession, have the new Church Order, have all the certificates of the land owned by the Donggala Church, have an opportunity to baptize Tajio and Lauje, the original tribes on the mountain of Tinombo in East Coastal Sulawesi, and last but not least – thanks be to God – have a strong relationship with EMS since 1977. May God from whom all blessings flow be with the big family of EMS and crown all its hard efforts with success for the glory of Lord Jesus Christ, now and forever more." (…)

Team Visit IV to the Protestant Church of the Palatinate (EKP) and The Protestant Church in Baden (EKiBa), April 2016

Benjamin Simon

The Team Members on Mission, Before and After

Everyone interested in becoming a part of the Team was asked to submit a personal statement on the meaning of mission as a part of the application process. In the course of the visit, this original understanding was challenged by the various experiences the Team made. (…) Here under you will find the Mission Statement each candidate had to articulate before the Team Visit.

- Bien Bangapadang (Protestant Church in South-East Sulawesi): Mission facilitates people from different churches to visit other churches in order to share ideas and experiences.
- Soulus Jeffrin (Basel Christian Church of Malaysia):
  I have found that mission is at the core of my ministry. In my teaching through Bible Studies, Youth Groups and in sermons, I emphasize doing mission throughout our life's journey. Without mission, the church can never grow.
- Lee, Byongho (Presbyterian Church in the Republic of Korea): Mission is best summed up in this phrase: Whatever you have done for one of the least of these Sisters and Brothers of mine, you did for me (cf. Matthew 25:40). I have deep interest in community mission at the local level. I myself participate in a ministry providing free meals to the elderly and homeless at lunch time.
- Lee, Hee Jeong (Presbyterian Church of Korea):
  As Jesus' disciple, I would like to be a missionary to Myanmar. I was there for a short time last summer. I visited several churches in Yangon and shared my testimony with them. I now understand that the meaning of "mission" is to share my beliefs, life and experience with people in the spirit of Jesus Christ.
- Samuel Odjelua (Presbyterian Church of Ghana):

My understanding of mission is that it is an organized effort for the propagation of the Christian faith, so that people will have life in its fullness.

- Willem J. Valentyn (Moravian Church in South Africa):
  Mission is to share the good news of the biblical principle that Jesus saves and that He is our Saviour.
- Rana Zankoul (Episcopal Church of Jerusalem and the Middle East): As Christians, we proclaim the good news of the Kingdom of God. We reflect the love and the light of Jesus Christ to others.
- Rainer Lamotte (Protestant Church of the Palatinate):
  Mission is to live and spread the Gospel. For me, the first step in mission is to listen to the other and to look at his / her life conditions, traditions, resources etc. Mission is communication. Mission is living together, sharing, acting in solidarity and practicing advocacy. Mission is convivence (Theo Sundermeier). Mission is participating in God's mission to the world. Mission is sharing, praying, singing, suffering and rejoicing together in the one world.
- Diks Pasande (Protestant Indonesian Church in Luwu / Protestant Church in Baden): Mission is encountering and sharing: encountering people from other cultures, traditions and religions, sharing our love and care in daily life. In that way we proclaim the kingdom of God, that is God's love to all human beings and creatures.
- Benjamin Simon (Protestant Church in Baden):
  Mission started with God. We are only salt and light. God is the one who brings conversion; we humans season and illumine the world by our deeds, actions and our solidarity with and for others.

Addressing the Questions: The Team at Work

1. How do the Protestant Churches in Baden (EKiBa) and the Palatinate (EKP) understand mission in today's world? Do they have mission statements? If so: what topics do these statements address?

The EKiBa and the EKP both understand mission in various ways. They see mission as a fulfilment of the will of God on earth. Their mission understanding finds expression in their initiatives to bring hope and care to all humanity. The emphasis on social services (i.e. diaconia), is in itself abundant evidence that both Churches are conscious about mission.

Unfortunately, both Churches lack a written manifesto which showcases their Mission and Vision Statements. We urge both Churches to develop specific Mission statements and make them visible in all areas of their operations.

Who are the agents of mission in the EKiBa and the EKP?

During its visits to the regions where the EKiBa and EKP are carrying out their mission, the Team was hosted by several institutions and attended many events, listening to a multitude of information from various sources and directly observing people who engage with human resource development, e.g. staff members of the "Evangelische Schule" and the "Evangelische Fachschule Bethlehem" in Karlsruhe or the EKiBa Head Office .We received leaflets describing various aspects of the Protestant Church in Baden. The EKiBa has three levels of organization, i.e.: (1) the congregation/parish, led by a parish council and minister(s) serving it, (2) the church district/deanery, led by a district synod, a district council and a superintendent (dean) and (3) the Regional Church "Evangelische Landeskirche in Baden", led by the Synod, the Bishop and the senior church officers. The EKiBa has over 1,23 million members and is organized in 25 church districts with total 690 congregations. There are 1.021 ministers working in congregations and about 32.000 employees are working in diaconal institutions, schools and Kindergartens.

The Team Visit further visited the Deaconess Hospital and Hospitz in Speyer, where the Team met various staff members. The Team Visit members attended Sunday worship in several congregations, both urban and rural, and visited the "Refugee Admission Facility" in Heidelberg, the Christival in Karlsruhe, and the Department of Mission and Ecumenism Landau.

Those working in the head offices, both in Baden and the Palatinate, in the various church districts, in parish offices, diaconal institutions, church-run schools and kindergartens and ordinary church members are all agents of mission. Nevertheless, when the members of Team Visit attended Sunday worship, whether in Baden or the Palatinate, they found only few church members in attendance. According to information received from pastors and elders, only some 5 to 10 % of the members actively attend Sunday worship and various activities of the church.

Therefore, the question arises: "How could the inactive members of church also become agents of mission?" The Team recommends that the churches encourage its active members by empowering them to be "mission multipliers". Further, the churches should be teaching their members an understanding of mission which is not connected with the understanding of mission in the 19th century. Mission is rather the work of God. We as agents of mission are salt and light (Matthew 5:13-16 / Missio Dei). This should be included in a mission statement.

3. What role does evangelization play and what forms of evangelization are deemed appropriate?

From our point of view, mission and evangelization are the same. The meaning of mission as God's mission to the world through the church is evangelization or spreading the good news. The meaning of evangelization is often defined too narrowly, limiting it to a process of Christianization process. Evangelization is not identical with Christianization.

Evangelization is a process by which we share the love of God and "the good news" with other people. As Baden Bishop Jochen Cornelius-Bundschuh expressed it at the Ecumenical Day: It is time for the church to push aside its triumphalist and arrogant actions. We learn from history that the church has done much damage in the name of Christianization. It used a "narrow proselytism", at the same time persecuting other believers, cultures and traditions.

Our visits to the varieties of activities and institutions have led us to new perspectives and understandings about what evangelization is. Evangelization is the heart of the church. Or even we might say that the Church is itself evangelization. Without evangelization, the church would not be church. It would rather be a kind of benevolent non-governmental organization (NGO).

During our activities saw that both the Baden Church and Palatinate Church implement the understandings of evangelization through many and various ways:

- By the diaconal, social and humanitarian services (diaconia, refugees and peace works, etc.)
- Education activities at various levels; particularly for the youth.
- Ecumenical activities through which the rich traditions of the various churches are shared.

During our visit, we also learned that the future of Church as an institution depends on its social services to others and its willingness to humbly open its hearts and doors to young people.

We are optimistic about the future of the churches in Europe, as long as they are willing to invite and encourage their youth to involve itself as much as possible in their various activities. Youth should be subjects, not only objects of church endeavour.

A critical observation: The Team found that in Europe, Christians are too rational, too busy with social activities but lacking in spirituality. In Asia and Africa, Christians are busy with rituals to the extent of being trapped their formality but lacking in social humanitarian interest and activities. Let us work in north and south to balance the two.

4. How are other religions seen vis-à-vis such central themes as salvation or redemption?

Salvation in Christ is a gift. It's not because of human kindness, nor because we deserved it but because of the grace and mercy of God. (…)

In diaconal work involving non-Christians, especially in Baden church, the non-Christian accept the assistance offered. Jihad, a Muslim refugee from Syria was also gave an account of being assisted by a Christian group. Jihad got along with the Christian community well, but still practices his Muslim faith. In our opinion, this is very important as a part of our lives as Christians. We express the love of God with sincerity to non-Christian people, not to convert them to Christianity but to show them the love of Jesus Christ in us (salt and light).

However, in a visit to the Protestant Church of St. Thomas, Rev. Zimmermann shared that they are also involved in helping the Muslim refugees. As a consequence, there have been some among them who accepted the Lord Jesus and were baptized.

5. Turning now to the current 500th Anniversary of the Reformation:

a)   In what way is the central Protestant doctrine "justification by faith alone" a part of the mission understandings of the EKiBa and the EKP?

Based on the doctrine of 'justification by faith alone', we believe that God loves all human beings. Therefore, the church should spread the love of God. It is out of this understanding that mission begins. Accordingly, faith is a fruit of God's love. The church's mission is God's mission, not a mission of the church itself (World Mission Conference, Willingen 1952). In this regard, churches carry out God's mission. The church's mission is nothing more than an expression of God's will.

b)   What is the foundation of the ethical teachings of the EKiBa and the EKP and how does this foundation relate to the core Reformation insight "by scripture alone"?

The foundation of ethical teachings is what Jesus teaches in Scripture. That's why we have to implement the teachings of Jesus in daily life. Just as we experienced in the "Diakonissen- Haus" in Speyer: "whatever you did to one of the least of these my brothers and sisters, you did to me." (Mt. 25, 40).

Further, we read in Matthew about the stranger who was accepted: Next door to the Refugee Admission Facility (Landeserstaufnahme-stelle) in Karlsruhe we met people from the Diaconia (Protestant) and Caritas (Roman Catholic) who cared for refugees in an ecumenical spirit. It was wonderful to see them cooperating so well. Nevertheless, we missed other denominations. What about the Orthodox or the Pentecostals?

c)   To what extent do the EKiBa and the EKP understand themselves to be in a process of ongoing, continual reformation?

Nowadays, the situation is rapidly changing, not only in Europe, but all over the world. One of the reasons is because of the increasing number of migrants and refugees. In the opinion of the Team, churches in Germany should help to solve this problem, treating refugees as their own brothers and sisters no matter what religion or cultural background they have. Further, injustice, poverty, corruption and conflicts take place throughout the world. The church as an agent of mission is called to be salt and light wherever it is needed to do so.

It would be very important to deepen the contacts to the many migrant churches within the areas of the EKiBa and the EKP, so that a continual ecumenical and intercultural exchange takes place.

This would be one expression of an ongoing, continual Reformation.

6. Are diaconal or social components a part of the mission concept of the EKiBa and the EKP? If so, what role do they play?

We believe that diaconal or social components are definitely a part of the mission concept of the two churches. They play a major role in fulfilling the mission concept of these two churches. By God's love and grace, we are enabled to do good deeds and be involved in the society around us. Social activities give hope to the continuity of Christianity.

a)   Youth Organisations: They are independent and draw in many volunteers. Through social activities, young people are encouraged to take part in the church. Through their participation, they share in fulfilling the mission of the church. (…)

Through social activities targeting the youth, such as the "Christival", new methods are employed to attract youth to participate and to adopt a positive outlook. They succeeded in attracting young people through live rock music, competitions similar to that of a famous game show etc.

b)		*Diaconia* was historically independent of the church, in order to obtain the financial support of the government. The motivation for having diaconia was the Christian ethics of life and the social situation in the 19th Century. It was seen as an implementation of the word of Jesus in Mathew. It is therefore derived from the Bible and is doing what Jesus did in his time.

Diaconal work is social and it plays a very important role in the mission of the church, because it is done in the spirit of the Christian faith. Also, it is doing the work that was first initiated by the church (such as feeding the hungry, giving shelter to those in need, caring for the elderly and the orphans, caring for the sick etc.).

(…) It is essential to recognize that all diaconal institutions (hospitz, hospitals, elderly homes, educational institutions, etc.) keep the spirit of Christ. All these institutions depict the Christian way of life and the biblical teaching of loving and accepting and helping our neighbours. This is the reason for having these institutions and doing the social work on the first place.

Educational institutions encourage students´ active Christian involvement in many social programs and projects. This can sometimes happen through field trips, camps, visits to the elderly homes, feeding homeless people and doing refugee work. Religion is a part of the music, literature, and art courses given to students. Moreover, these educational institutions are in partnership with Christian child care facilities. Spirituality is exercised in these institutions, which in turn play an important role in the mission concept of the churches.

c)		*Refugee social work:* The social activity of helping asylum seekers through social work and counselling for refugees is a task that brings many people closer to the church. For example, caritas, derived from the Christian faith, tries to solve health and social problems and to help Christian refugees through counselling to cope with others. Further examples of social activity for refugees is the donation of clothing, the encouraging of creative work among refugee children and adults as well as teaching skills such as knitting and learning German language, thus helping them to be more effective socially.

7. All of those involved in the Team Visits, be it the visitors or be it those being visited, are part and parcel of the "Evangelical Mission in Solidarity". What is the connection between "mission" and "solidarity" in the EKiBa and the EKP? In what way is this connection being lived out in its ongoing work?

In our experiences in the EkiBa and the EKP, 'Mission' was not merely living together with all people in Germany, but getting deeply involved with them. Many churches and institutions continue to embrace their sufferings with open and warm hearts. In this process, churches act in solidarity with many denominations from all over the world.

(…) Why did we have the ecumenical service first, before experiencing the various works of mission in the EkiBa and the EKP? The idea that we should first have had time to be humbled through worship. After meeting God in worship, we can better listen to other's voices and sympathize other's pain. In other words, we must have solidarity to understand the diversity of God's creation. (…)

However, migration and refugee movements area worldwide phenomenon. Therefore, Germany needs new solutions and inspirations from all over the world. That is the reason why German churches need relationships and partnerships with churches and denominations across the world. In this regard, mission and solidarity have an inseparable relation. (…)

Accordingly, we see that 'mission in solidarity' is not only about delivering the Gospel to the world in a narrow sense, but also getting involved with all persons peacefully as brothers and sisters. This is the wisdom and method for living together in the diverse creation of God.

In conclusion, 'mission in solidarity' is summed up in this phrase: 'And we know that God causes all things to work together for good to those who love God, to those who are called according to His purpose.' (Romans 8:28)

8. In the end: What is the overall effect of missionary endeavour as undertaken in and by the EKiBa and the EKP?

Having visited and attended various gatherings, diaconal undertakings, initiatives and being in discussions with various role players, we have seen that both the Protestant Church in Baden and the Protestant Church in the Palatinate are serious about reaching out to make the world a better place for all.

The model of Jesus is to minister to spirit, body and soul. Jesus is God's mission to the world. Jesus reaches out unconditionally to an imperfect world full of sin, pain and hopelessness. His purpose was to restore the image of mankind and creation. (…)

During the days of the Team Visit, we were filled with gratitude and appreciation for the well-structured, highly dedicated and motivated diaconal mission work that the EKiBa and the EKP are engaged in. Not all churches around the globe are so fortunate as to enjoy the positive working relationship between church and government which makes this possible. (…)

The Church proves to us that we cannot light a candle on our own and expects that it will burn in stormy and windy conditions. By cooperating with other churches (ecumenism) much more can be achieved. (…)

PART 3: THAT THEY MAY HAVE LIFE, AND HAVE IT ABUNDANTLY

Workshop:
Reading the Bible through the Eyes of Another

Gabriele Mayer

For many years "Bible-sharing" has become an important element of many ecumenical international encounters. Therefore it is nothing unusual to offer a time of Bible-sharing during the course of this symposium, where four teams reflected on their learnings while visiting EMS member churches in other parts of the world.

What kind of theological learning takes place when different people listen to the same Bible passage but with different ears and different eyes – and start sharing their observations of the text, start talking about life experiences?

This Bible-sharing was actually offered and shaped according the EMS FOCUS 2015-2019 "Life in Fullness for All – Mission in Solidarity". The international Bible Project has an emphasis on bringing together grass-roots groups "reading the Bible through the eyes of another". 90 groups around the globe had registered in early 2016. Tandems were formed where two groups from different backgrounds, cultures, languages, church traditions were invited to read the same Bible passages and send their observations and insights to the respective tandem partner. These groups did not travel physically, but rather they struggled to overcome communication barriers still existing in geographical regions due to lacking a computer or unreliable energy or limited access to English/Spanish language skills. Nevertheless they made efforts to seek ways in building bridges to a group they only slowly got acquainted with.

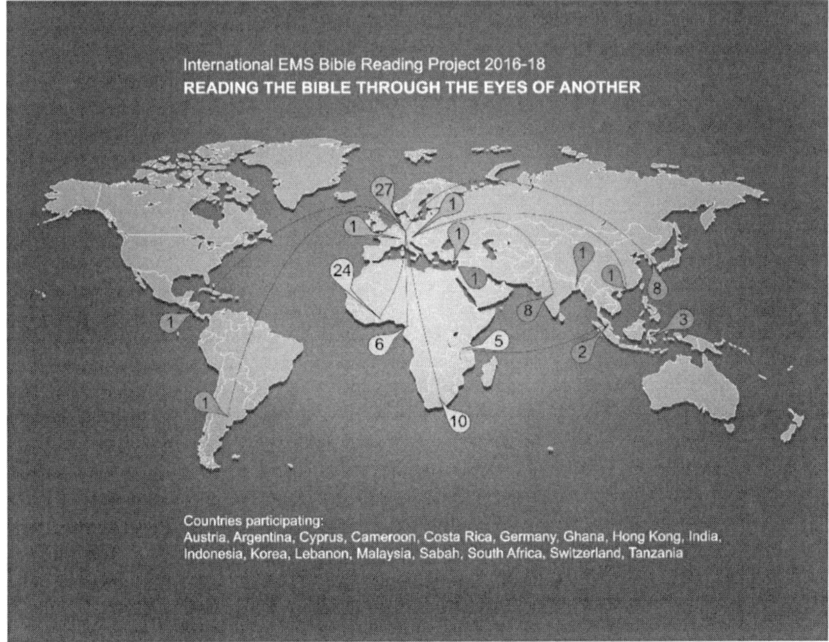

Symposium

On June 8 a plenary session enabled the participants of the Symposium to leave the roles of listeners or presenters, and actually interacted with one another in small groups. The suggested Bible passage is unfamiliar, rarely preached upon, but among the Bible reading groups it became quite popular.

Wondering why? This Bible passage addresses experiences and topics that many groups from African and Asian countries are quite familiar with: life and death situation, exclusion due to sickness, military threats, fighting for survival. And last not least: "life in fullness for all" – how can that be shared in a life threatening war like situation?

2. Kings 7: 3-11 (NRSV)

3 Now there were four leprous men outside the city gate, who said to one another, "Why should we sit here until we die?

4 If we say, 'Let us enter the city', the famine is in the city and we shall die there; but if we sit here, we shall also die.

Therefore, let us desert to the Aramean camp; if they spare our lives, we shall live; and if they kill us, we shall but die."

5 So they arose at twilight to go to the Aramean camp, but when they came to the edge of the Aramean camp, there was no one there at all.

6 For the Lord had caused the Aramean army to hear the sound of chariots and of horses, the sound of a great army, so that they had said to one another, 'The king of Israel has hired the kings of the Hittites and the kings of Egypt to fight against us.'

7 So they fled away in the twilight and abandoned their tents, their horses, and their donkeys, leaving the camp just as it was and fled for their lives.

8 When these leprous men had come to the edge of the camp, they went into a tent, ate and drank, carried off silver, gold, and clothing, and went and hid them. Then they came back, entered another tent, carried off things from it, and went and hid them.

9 Then they said to one another, "What we are doing is wrong. This is a day of good news; if we are silent and wait until the morning light, we will be found guilty; therefore let us go and tell the king's household."

10 So they came and called to the gatekeepers of the city, and told them,

"We went to the Aramean camp, but there was no one to be seen or heard there, nothing but the horses tied, the donkeys tied, and the tents as they were."

11 Then the gatekeepers called out and proclaimed it to the king's household.

A method from South Africa

This methodology was developed during the apartheid era when congregations did not have sufficient trained theologians but an urgent need to read the Bible through the eyes of suffering people. They longed to uphold their faith in the midst of an unjust racist system, with severe human rights violations and poverty that forced them to fight for survival.

They developed a method that called for attentive listening to the Bible text, to listen with their life concerns and their need to share with fellow Christians what they could do as joint endeavours to improve their life circumstances.

Transferring the method to Bad Boll

Sitting in a big circle this Bible passage was read twice and quite slowly, listened and meditated and reflected upon by all the participants. Then, in four smaller groups, people started to share life experiences sparked by the Bible passage. They exchanged insights from their faith journey. They asked questions to get a better understanding of the other's context. And gradually they identified commonalities, but also differences which aspect of the Bible passages became important to the individual participant - and other aspects were dropped. It became obvious that the participants embody differing attitudes of listening, of sharing, of talking about personal and communal experiences – and about spiritual insights.

Bible-sharing in seven steps – as outlined in the centre of each small group

1. Opening with prayer or song
2. Listening to the Bible passage
3. Giving voice to the biblical text
4. Meditating in silence
5. Sharing insights
6. Acting together
7. Closing with prayer or song

How does learning take place?

The dynamic of this workshop embraced a variety of sensory perceptions and different 'learning' moments, e.g.

Step 1: the facilitator invites a shy person to pray who was not very visible until that moment.

Step 2: being introduced to learning to understand our own body as a music instrument that can resonate with the biblical text. Listening not primarily with our mind but with our body memory.

Step 3: seeing the emergence of a new text patterns and learning which words resonated with the fellow listeners.

Step 4: feeling the calming and comforting minutes of silence in the midst of a busy conference.

Step 6: The most visible form emerged when the small international groups were asked to find an expression with their bodies and very few words on how the "good news" can be expressed. One group actually was seeking access through the window. Another group formed a frozen picture. A third group shouted the good message in a loud voice…

The symposium intended to reflect on "lessons learnt" brought together by four team visits.

The Bible Project offers a different platform for mutual learning processes: by listening to one another in an intercultural setting. Therefore getting acquainted with the methodology of the EMS Bible Project offers an additional point of entry to intercultural theological learning.

                                  Gabriele Mayer

Photo: EMS

"But where the spirit of the Lord is, there is freedom" – Sermon on 2 Corinthians 3:17

Frank O. July / Affifa Rose Hermle[1]

Bishop July: Grace be with you and peace in our Lord Jesus Christ. Amen.

What is lovely and special about this day, in the world-wide church, is that we can stand together on this pulpit and exchange our views. A Catholic theologian born in Pakistan and a Protestant bishop, together, here in Wuerttemberg. This is indeed something special, but it does belong to Pentecost that we exchange our experiences.

Dear Sisters and Brothers, dear Congregation, Pentecost is a festival where we in a very special way, year after year, pray for the presence of the Spirit of God to guide us every day of our lives. Yesterday we preached in our churches and heard how God renews us. As Jesus said: I send you my Spirit to comfort you, and I send you my Spirit of mercy. The Spirit of Mercy, the Spirit of Clarity and the Spirit of Truth - sent guide us in our differences. It strengthens and blesses us, enabling us to break new ground in our everyday lives and at the same time constantly calling us together, as different people in one community, as is today the case. What a very impressive and touchable experience.

The sermon text comes from the second letter to the Corinthians, and is similar to today's motto: The Lord is Spirit. Where the Spirit of the

---

[1] Dr. h.c. Frank O. July is Bishop of the Evangelical-Lutheran Church in Württemberg.
Mrs. Affifa Rose Hermle is a Pastoral Assistant at the Catholic Church in the town of Markgröningen in Württemberg.

Lord is, there is freedom. Freedom is a big word. A word linked with many ideas, ideals and personal convictions. But freedom is also a word which in the history of humankind has again and again been soiled and stained. Some promises of freedom have indeed become law in the world. Some liberation struggles have fallen into the hands of those with who use power and terror unscrupulously. Because of that, it is important when we speak of freedom as Christians that we remind ourselves of the witness of Martin Luther; that freedom comes from Christ and returns to him, as it is bound to him. Freedom is an expression of the community with Christ. When the Son of God has made you free, you are really free. For us as Christians, freedom is connected with Jesus Christ.

A few weeks ago, I attended the Assembly of the Worldwide Lutheran Church in Namibia. There we were gathered under the theme ``Liberated by God's grace''. There I saw how deeply Christians from Asia, Africa, North and South America, but also from Europe and other parts of the world, experience freedom; God's grace in their personal lives and in the respective contexts of their various societies and contexts.

For all of us, freedom and grace are surely not abstract words or titles, but have to be constantly defined in our daily life, in our world and in our society. For some, freedom means resisting when they are oppressed or pressured in their societies; or at the very least to believe and have faith in the redemptive power of Jesus Christ. It may mean breaking new ground, speaking out against the rise of nationalism in Europe and elsewhere, or against some role-understandings in society. It may mean standing up for greater justice in our countries. For educational justice, as a woman of Liberia told me, for more education so that we may better understand the Gospel, and in so doing, becoming better able to speak and present the Gospel in her church.

A Youth delegate from Papua New Guinea said: ``God gave me freedom to be an advocate in our church so that young people can also make their voices heard. We want to protect this God-given freedom. We want to receive this freedom of Christ as a special gift and protect it like the apple of our eye. The freedom given by God in Christ always allows us new beginnings. We know that we sometimes come to very different judgments and conclusions in listening to the Word of God and His freedom, yet, the Spirit of God calls us together, as different as we and our various churches may be, in the diversity of our lives, to endure, stay on the way and to listen to each another. This freedom cannot be cornered by racism and hate speech, by national self-agility and exclusion. This Christ-given-freedom also knows of our daily endangerment and of the refractions in our personal nd in our everyday lives.

But where the Spirit of the Lord is, there is freedom. Dear Mrs. Hermle, the Spirit of Pentecost also accompanies you in your perceptions, also in your home country Pakistan. Can you perhaps lead us further by explaining how you experience the Holy Spirit in Pakistan and here in Germany, that is to say what the Pentecost Spirit means for you?

***Mrs. Affia Rose Hermle:** In Pakistan, where I come from, Christians are a small minority. Pakistan is the second largest Islamic country worldwide. Islam is a state religion and Islamic law, the Sharia, is the basis of jurisprudence. Instruction in Islam is obligatory in all schools. As a Christian, however, you should not have a good mark in it.*

Some time ago, a Christian pupil from Lahore was in great distress because she had a very good mark. The authorities wanted to force her to become a Muslima. She had to flee with her family. In Pakistan, religious persecution is the order of the day. Each year, several hundred Christian girls are kidnapped by Muslims, Islamized by force and compelled to marry a Muslim. The fact that Christians are regarded as unclean or untouchable by the majority of Muslims unfortunately does not protect them. Christians dare not resist such verbal violence. They must choose every word most carefully or else they will be charged with blasphemy. Yet the blasphemy laws in Pakistan were originally neutral and intended to protect all religions.

In 1982, the deliberate dishonouring of the Koran meant life imprisonment. In 1986, the death penalty and lifelong imprisonment were introduced for making derogatory statements about the Prophet Muhammed. These Pakistani blasphemy laws have fundamentally changed the situation of the Christians. They now live in constant fear. Again and again it happens that Christians are accused of blasphemy simply to get rid of them. Before the introduction of these laws it was different. I used to live with my family in a Muslim area. This was unusual even then, because Christians usually lived in their own ghettos. For Christians, only menial work is available, so my parents were poor. As children, we were often discriminated against. At school we were not welcome. Both teachers and classmates insulted us by calling us "Kafir", meaning "unbelievers". We have accepted it as the price of our faith. However, we did not fear prison or death. We did not know the violence and persecution we know today. I remember exactly how my mother openly discussed her faith with Muslims. Today she would expect to receive the death penalty for it. Yet despite all dangers and difficulties, Christians hold fast to their faith. For Christians in Pakistan, faith is an essential part of everyday life. Whatever they say or do - God is always there. Faith gives them strength and courage to live. God's Spirit gives them internal freedom despite persecution and discrimination. It is not easy for them. They suffer. They are prosecuted. They are tortured, sometimes killed. They need our prayers and they need our support.

July: That is why in our Protestant Church in Wuerttemberg there are regular and ongoing prayers for Christians in other countries who are subject to persecution and threat. Through this, we feel our connectedness with them in the Spirit of Christ. We are called upon not to treat our sisters and brothers in the world with indifference, but to support them in their struggle for freedom. We should be thankful that we live in a country where we can enjoy religious freedom. External freedom and personal freedom belong together, but the societal structures as well. Pakistan is a country known for cheap labour, where many people work in the textile industry, where women and children hardly have the possibility of experiencing freedom. How is it with external freedom or with economic independence?

Hermle: *Many Christians work in the textile industry. As second-class citizens only low-grade work is available. Christians work as street cleaners, rubbish collectors, sewage workers and sewer cleaners. Many also work as unqualified agricultural labourers* *for the major landowners in Pakistan, or as workers in brick factories. Even children work at 45 degrees Celsius from morning to night in the blazing sun. Similar conditions prevail in the textile industry. Despite the boiling heat, garment workers often have to work with poisonous fabrics. Many of them have problems breathing and have skin diseases. Among Christians, tuberculosis and hepatitis are much more widespread because medical treatment in Pakistan must be paid for in cash and they cannot afford it. My sister, cousins and nephews have worked in such textile factories. At 5 a.m. they are picked up by the factory bus in their villages and neighbourhoods. Travelling to work takes 3 hours one way. For a 13 hour day they receive a wage of 50 Euros per month and are being beaten for making even the slightest mistake.*

July: The General Secretary of the Lutheran World Federation has coined the phrase ``The Reformation became a World citizen.'' That means that the message of freedom, which we have rediscovered and share today with Christians all over the world, shall accompany us worldwide. This is particularly true during this Reformation Jubilee in the year 2017. It is important for us to emphasize education once again. And today, thinking of the Mission Festival which we are now celebrating, our ``Landesmissionsfest'', and also of the ongoing mission work, to emphasize that mission includes medical assistance. We have just heard about the difficulties in health care and education. Mission work that confesses Christ through medical and educational assistance shows solidarity with the gospel of freedom for the children of God. Our Reformer Johannes Brenz, who lies buried under the pulpit of this church, called for education for boys and for the girls as long as 500 years ago. Education, so that people can experience freedom by perceiving the Word of God for themselves. Dear Mrs. Hermle, you yourself have contributed to the construction of two new schools in Pakistan. What experience have you had with the theme, 'Education and Freedom' in this regard?

Hermle*: In Pakistan, education is particularly important for Christians. It is their only chance to escape social discrimination. But good education is very expensive in Pakistan and is often denied to Christians. Good education is usually only* *available in private schools. These demand high admission and school fees. Most Christians cannot afford them. Unfortunately, this is also often the case for schools built with aid funds from the West. In state schools, teaching is often irregular and the quality very low. In state schools Christians are often discriminated against. They are beaten, forced to sit separately, and usually they receive bad marks. Because of all this and more, I founded the association PaxVobis twelve years ago, which has given itself the goal of changing this situation. We now run two schools in Pakistan with over 300 pupils. These are schools founded by the poor for the poor. Most children do not pay school fees. Teachers work for a symbolic salary which is not enough to live on. Here the children are taught in English. Normally it is only schools for the rich that offer this in Pakistan. One of the schools is located in a Christian slum where there was no school before. When the school opened a father said, "Into our darkness light has come." Some time ago, a boy was admitted to a distant state school. There he was abused every day. He has a hole in his cheek. A teacher once pushed a pencil through his cheek. Now he is glad that he can learn without fear and live his faith. The second school is located on the edge of a slum and is attended by both Muslim and Christian children. Here children learn to respect and support each other. They pray together, learn together and help each other. Sometimes they even bring food for each other. We are convinced that children who receive a good school education, as well as attention and appreciation, will think more freely and live together more peacefully.*

July: Yes, the Catholic Pastoral Assistant and the Protestant Bishop are indeed listening to each other and sharing their experiences. For me, a moment in which we gain a sense of our calling in freedom, that is the freedom in Christ. We are called to seek the centre in our relation to Jesus Christ, to experience new fellowship. In that fellowship, we should listen to the sufferings of others, and intercede for their situations, praying together for God's blessing and guidance for us all. The presence of the Holy Spirit, as I said in the beginning, is what we pray or plea for at Pentecost. The presence of the Spirit binds us together in our differences again and again, as it does today and even with us. Amen.

> **Hermle**: *The freedom of Christians in Pakistan is restricted in many ways. But freedom cannot simply be restricted by external circumstances. God can give us an inner freedom that cannot be restricted. Jesus has won for us a victory which no one can take away. Paul says, "Who will separate us from the love of Christ? Tribulation or fear or persecution or hunger or nakedness or danger or sword?" (Romans 8:35) Nothing in the world can separate us from the love of God. Where we recognize this there is freedom. Where we unite in prayer like the Apostles did and open ourselves to the Holy Spirit, the chains of fear and despair are broken. There we learn "the glorious freedom of the children of God" (Romans 8:21). AMEN.*

Impressions from the Symposium – Photos: Waltz/EMS

Communiqué

of the EMS Symposium 2017

That they may have life, and have it abundantly. (John 10:10)

1. Introduction

From June 5-9, 2017, 37 participants from different EMS member churches and mission societies, EMS Mission Council, EMS Secretariat, and selected external experts gathered in Stuttgart and at the Protestant Academy in Bad Boll. Their purpose was to share insights with regard to the many and diverse mission concepts operative within the EMS Fellowship, and to enter into an exchange as to which avenues of mission might best be pursued within the EMS Community in the future.

The basis for this discussion were the four "EMS Team Visits" which took place in 2015-16. At that time, mixed teams of different nationalities, representing the diversity of EMS Member Churches and Mission Societies, visited the Presbyterian Church of Ghana (PCG), the Church of South India (CSI), the Indonesian Protestant Church in Donggala (GPID) or the Protestant Churches in the Palatinate (EKP) and in Baden (EKiBa). Their task was to "mirror" the mission approaches in these respective churches and to present their findings to the Symposium. Other participants contributed insights gleaned from their own missiological research. This three-year process, a high point in the EMS Focus, was a contribution of the EMS to the 200th Anniversary of the Basel Mission and the 500th Anniversary of the Protestant Reformation.

The Symposium was held in conjunction with the "Festival of the Worldwide Church and Mission" of the Evangelical-Lutheran Church in Württemberg: As a public lecture within that Festival, and as the opening lecture of the Symposium, Dr. Rima Nasrallah of Beirut presented her reflections on "Mission, Religion and Values in a Fragmented World". Nasrallah suggested replacing the concept of "mission through expansion" with a "mission through networks" as a response to an increasing culture of fear: Inviting a stranger to become part of your network can become a door-opener to gain access to the network of this stranger. In this way, persons who otherwise would have remained unknown can share their life concerns.

Setting the tone for what was then to follow, EMS General Secretary Jürgen Reichel and EMS Mission and Partnership Department Head Dr. Kerstin Neumann reflected upon the practice of mission as delineated in the EMS constitution and on the basis of recent challenges faced by the EMS Community.

What happened when, in the course of the EMS Team Visits, complete strangers were exposed to cultures and churches so different from their own? This question was taken up by Prof. Dr. Theo Sundermeier (Heidelberg) who introduced the participants into his "Hermeneutics of the Stranger". For Sundermeier, strangeness is always a relational term which can be transformed into a force for positive action once a level of "*convivence*" is reached.

The "relevance of our roots", that is to say the relationship between mission endeavors of the past and those of the present was unfolded from an European and from an African perspective by Dr. Benedict Schubert (Basel), and Emmanuel Tettey (Accra), while Prof. Dr. Andreas Heuser (Basel) turned to the present, submitting a case study regarding "New Dynamics in Mission and Christianity".

After the presentation of "Highlights from the Team Visits" by their respective participants, the Symposium's focus turned to strategies and action. Four working groups reflected on "Doing Mission in different Contexts": The Christian-Jewish context, the Christian-Muslim context, the context of Christian minorities and the context of youth in mission. As a practical exercise, Dr. Gabriele Mayer (Stuttgart) led the participants into an exploration of 2nd Kings 7:3-11 by using the method of "Reading the Bible with the Eyes of Another".

During the Symposium, it became more and more evident that the mission approaches used in the various EMS member churches are in fact quite diverse, and that a high level of sensitivity is needed in order to remain open for the abundant life promised by Jesus Christ to his disciples.

2. Today's Challenges

The Preamble of the EMS constitution defines the purpose of EMS as "uniting churches and mission societies as equal partners in the common witness to the Gospel of Jesus Christ." The witness of the four Team Visits formed the basis for reflecting mission and addressing challenges.

We affirm enriching diversity within the EMS Fellowship and that the experience of personal relationships counts. This suggests that mission be viewed as a search for new community, indicating that we can overcome geographical distances, live with cultural and theological differences and bring together those at the center of political and economic power with those at the margins (EMS Agenda 2014-2020).

Transferring this experience into the whole of the EMS Community is of importance considering the challenges we face on the global scale:

- The ideological misuse of religion as a support system for exclusion and oppression.

- The increasingly varied faith expressions ranging from secular skepticism towards religion to a Christian culture that affirms authoritative leadership and is even committed at times to a confrontational evangelization style.

Common history and shared values are a firm basis for talking about, living and dreaming such togetherness. This includes the open discussion of challenges and topics that may bring controversial opinions to the fore. Some examples may be mentioned:

- How much religious dedication can be expected from Ecumenical Youth Volunteers being sent to EMS Member Churches?

- What types of evangelization projects can be considered to be eligible for receiving funding from EMS?

Other areas that may require a revisiting of our common approach are interfaith dialogue and the role of diaconal work in mission. Along this line, the Team Visits and the Symposium were carried out in a culture of hospitality and mutual trust respecting the identity and the freedom of the other.

3. The Team Visits as an Instrument for Mirroring Mission

At the heart of the four EMS Team Visits was Item Six of the EMS Mission Statement as formulated in Chennai in 2003: *"We witness the Gospel of Jesus Christ at all our respective places in an inviting and faithful way. The experience of being strangers to each other in encounters and in exchange across borders helps us to rediscover the Gospel in new ways."* Towards this end, the teams were deliberately composed not of "outside experts" coming as it were to evaluate the church being visited, but rather of "strangers", that is to say persons experienced ecumenically, but not familiar with the visited church. The necessary expertise was provided by team members coming from the hosting church. Though the visiting strangers sometimes asked questions which proved to be difficult, even challenging, in every case such situations could in the end be used productively for a greater understanding of the given church's situation. Particularly valuable were situations in which persons coming from contexts in which there is great freedom to evangelize openly were exposed to contexts in which this is not possible.

These experiences were deepened and qualified in the lecture given by Dr. Theo Sundermeier. He emphasized that the stranger is always seen in relation to that which is familiar, and can be perceived as a threat to the existing social order. At the same time, he indicated that the stranger can serve as a catalyst for dialogue, particularly in the sense of coming to be more familiar with each other (exchange of information) and learning how to co-exist peacefully (respect for the values and ethical standards of each other). In our own discussion, we added that the guest has a special status, remembering the words of Hebrews 13:2: "Do not neglect to show hospitality to strangers, for by doing that some have entertained angels without knowing it."

4. Mission in the EMS Community in Different Contexts

Context sensitivity is central in the EMS-Fellowship. Therefore, in different workshops, we tried to look at four specific contexts which are relevant for EMS members in their mission today: the Christian-

Jewish context, the Christian-Muslim context, the context of Christian minorities in their respective larger societies, and the context of youth in mission.

A context-sensitive mission is always an *ecumenical endeavor* which EMS Members do together with other churches and denominations in a given context. Only the local churches can determine the content and form of their mission, while the larger community of churches and missions is invited to support this mission.

a. While the *Jewish-Christian context* is more important in some geographical areas, and less important in others, we agree that our Christian faith is deeply rooted in the Jewish faith: Jews and Christians are sharing important parts of their Holy Scriptures, and the ultimate hope in God's Kingdom. God's calling of the church from different nations through Jesus Christ is strongly linked to God's election of the Jewish people.

We recognize that for some of us, the Jewish-Christian relation is overshadowed by the Israeli-Palestinian conflict, while others feel the deep need to respond to centuries of persecution of the Jews at the hands of Christians, mostly in Europe. In spite of this, and for Christ's sake, we can work together for justice and peace in the Holy Land, first of all strengthening our local Palestinian and Arab Christian brothers and sisters in this work. At the same time, we are called to fight anti-Semitism, hence making Jews feel safe and a part of our respective societies worldwide.

b. The *Christian-Muslim context* is a relevant context for many EMS members. Wherever Christians live together with Muslims, they encounter God's image in their Muslim neighbors and God's abounding love to them on a daily basis. In the dialogue of life, Christians share their faith with these Muslim neighbors in a natural way. Christian virtues like forgiveness, integrity, and supporting the needy are essential in this dialogue of life. In our relations with and witness to Muslims, we need to be trustworthy, open and honest. There must not be any hidden agenda.

c. In some geographical regions of the EMS community, Christians are only a small numerical minority of their societies. While the call to mission is universal, any *minority context* teaches us that mission, ultimately, is God's own initiative in which we can only participate. In some contexts, we focus on different aspects of a holistic mission, such as provision of education, social services, and good neighborhood, trusting that through these ways, God will draw people to himself.

The EMS community shows solidarity with Christian minorities, supporting them in their advocacy for equal citizenship. EMS churches and missions in a majority situation can learn a lot about interfaith dialogue from churches in a minority situation.

d. The context *of youth in mission* is a core issue for all EMS member churches. While we may have a variety of definitions of who is "Youth" – in a broader sense including age groups from 13 till 30 years – we recognize that young people are involved in mission in various ways. They are the future *and* present of our churches. Therefore, it is important to give youth greater attention and to offer space for their involvement.

5. Topics for further reflection in the EMS Fellowship

The Symposium participants recommend the following:

a) Christian / Jewish Context

- Working together for justice and peace in the Holy Land, through strengthening our local Palestinian and Arab Christian brothers and sisters in their struggle for peace and in their respective interfaith relations.
- Fighting anti-Semitism and doing whatever we can to make Jews feel safe wherever they live, promoting dialogue and encounter between Christians and Jews.

b) Christian / Muslim Context

- Promoting interpersonal encounters and/or dialogues between Christians and Muslims.
- Keeping the relationship open and staying connected with each other in an attitude of tolerance.
- Equipping our youth with a solid foundation in the Christian faith.

- Increasing our sharing of "best practice" examples of Christian Muslim dialogue in the EMS fellowship.

c) Christian Minorities and Indirect Approach to Mission

- Churches living in a minority situation are generally compelled to relate to more dominant religious groups with humility, even to the extent of bearing injustices without complaint. This experience should inform those churches living in contexts in which they themselves form the dominant culture, so that they themselves treat the minorities in their midst with respect and understanding.
- EMS Member Churches and Missions shall sit at the table and learn from each other how and where direct mission efforts from outside can be a threat for Christians in minority situations.

d) Youth in Mission

- Strengthening the presence of youth in today's church by creating space for youth through youth encounters and guaranteeing youth representation not only in the General Meeting but also on the Mission Council (with a seat or at least with an observer status).
- Supporting and expanding youth volunteer exchange in accordance with the EMS Youth Policy
- In order to further the connectedness of our churches, both now and in the future, increasing opportunities for the exchange of students during their theological training.

With regard to all of the above, we stress the importance of living our lives as letters of Christ, "written not with ink but with the Spirit of the living God, not on tablets of stone but on tablets of human hearts" (2. Cor. 3:3).

The Contributors

Rev. Heike Bosien is the executive director of Service for Mission, Ecumenical Relations and Development (DiMOE). The DiMOE team is responsible for global learning in congregations of the Evangelical Lutheran Church in Württemberg and at state schools in Württemberg. She is member of the EKD advisory commission for Worldwide Oikoumene and served in the Central Committee of the World Council of Churches from 1997-2013.

Rev. Riley Edwards-Raudonat, originally from the United States, has lived and worked in Germany since 1975. Currently, he is the EMS Africa Liaison Secretary, relating to churches in Ghana, Nigeria, South Sudan and South Africa. A pastor of the Evangelical-Lutheran Church in Wuerttemberg, he has served congregations in Oberkollbach and Ravensburg. Via EMS, he worked with rural congregations in Northern Ghana from 1988-95, his church host there being the Presbyterian Church of Ghana.

Rev. Dr. Uwe Gräbe works at the EMS Secretariat in Stuttgart as Middle East Liaison Secretary, and as Executive Secretary of the Evangelical Association for the Schneller Schools. Before, he was the Provost of the German Protestant Institutions in Israel, Palestine, and Jordan, based in Jerusalem. His research fields include Middle Eastern Christianity, contextual Palestinian theology and questions of Jewish-Christian dialogue.

Dr. Gabriele Mayer works at the EMS Secretariat in Stuttgart as Head of Women and Gender Unit and Secretary for Intercultural Theology and Learning. She is the editor of OUR VOICES published annually by the International EMS Women's Network in English, German and Indonesian. She is also responsible for the International EMS Bible Reading Project with participating groups from all EMS member churches in Asia, Africa and Europe.

Dr. Rima Nasrallah van Saane is the assistant professor of Practical Theology at the Near East School of Theology (NEST) in Beirut, with a particular focus on liturgical-ritual studies and Eastern churches. The NEST is the major theological institution for the formation of Protestant pastors in Lebanon, Syria, and Jordan.

Rev. Dr. Kerstin Neumann is the Deputy General Secretary of EMS and works as Head of Department for Mission and Partnership. Before joining EMS two years ago, she taught Religion and Philosophy at Tamilnadu Theological Seminary in Madurai, South India. One focus of interest in India was the interfaith dialogue.

Rev. Jürgen Reichel has been EMS General Secretary since 2013. Previously, he was Head of the Policy Department at the Protestant Development Services (EED – Evangelischer Entwicklungsdienst) in Bonn, Germany and Vice-Chair of the German NGO-Umbrella Organization VENRO. In the 1990's, he lived with his wife and four children in Venezuela, where he served – via the Evangelical Church in Germany – as pastor of the German-speaking Protestant Church in that country. His ordination is with the Lutheran Church in Bavaria, Germany.

Rev. Dr. Benedict Schubert, former teacher of grassroots leaders and pastors in Angola, then study secretary at mission 21 and lecturer in Missiology at Basel University, with his wife responsible for the student residence Theologisches Alumneum in Basel and pastor at the St Peter's Reformed Church; co-founder and member of the Community Don Camillo (based in Montmirail near Neuchâtel, Switzerland).

Rev. Dr. Benjamin Simon, former lecturer in Systematic Theology and Missiology at Makumira University College/Tanzania and Secretary for mission and ecumenism in the Protestant Church in Baden, Germany. Since 2016 Professor of Ecumenical Missiology at the WCC's Ecumenical Institute, Bossey, Geneva, and editor of the International Review of Mission (IRM).

Prof. em. Dr. Dr. h.c. Theo Sundermeier: Taught for 11 years in Southern Africa at different theological seminaries. In 1975 became professor of Theology of the History of Religions at Bochum University. From 1983 until retirement he served as professor of History of Religion and Missiology in the theology faculty of Heidelberg University and in the faculty for Oriental Studies and Studies of the Ancient World. Research emphasis: tribal religions, Christian art worldwide, intercultural hermeneutics.

Emmanuel Kwame Tettey is a member of the Presbyterian Church of Ghana and has been very active in the EMS Fellowship in various capacities, including serving as an ecumenical youth volunteer, delegate to the EMS General Meeting and a leader of the EMS International Youth Network. He holds a Master of Arts in Theology and Mission from the Akrofi-Christaller Institute of Theology, Mission and Culture and works with the Presbyterian Interfaith Research and Resource Centre in Accra as a research assistant. His areas of interest include holistic Christian mission in a multi-religious context.

***

We give thanks to all those who helped put the articles of this book into proper English – be it the British, American, or South African version of this language: Elaine Griffiths, Riley Edwards-Raudonat, and Gregson Jonathan Erasmus.

Beiträge zur Missionswissenschaft / Interkulturellen Theologie
hrsg. von Dieter Becker und Henning Wrogemann

Barbara Gierull
„Evangelisch-in-Jerusalem" im interreligiösen Dialog
Fragen bezüglich des interreligiösen Dialogs vor Ort – gewollt, gebraucht oder entbehrlich?
Evangelische Christen deutscher Sprache kommen als temporär Entsandte der Evangelischen Kirche Deutschlands (EKD) auch mit dem Auftrag zu einem interreligiösen Dialog nach Jerusalem. Die Stadt Jerusalem stellt mit den dortigen politischen, sozialen, kulturellen, gesellschaftlichen Gegebenheiten den Rahmen für diesen Dialog. Auch neue inhaltliche Aspekte werden in das Dialoggeschehen eingebracht, wie bspw. Jerusalem als Heilige Stadt der drei Weltreligionen Judentum – Christentum – Islam, Biblische Geschichte, Historie, aber auch Jerusalem als Nagelprobe für eine Zweistaatenlösung Israel – Palästina. Vor diesem Hintergrund beschreibt die Arbeit die Besonderheiten des interreligiösen Dialogs seitens der evangelischen Christen deutscher Sprache in Jerusalem.
Bd. 40, 2017, 444 S., 49,90 €, br., ISBN 978-3-643-13854-5

Heinrich Balz
Warum Robinson nicht zu Hause blieb
Europäische Expansion, Welterkundung und Mission
Robinson Crusoe, der 1719 erschienene Roman von Daniel Defoe, hat als Jugendbuch weltweite Wirkung gehabt: die Geschichte vom erfinderisch tätigen Menschen, der auf einsamer Insel die menschliche Kultur neu aufbaut. Auch seine Botschaft für erwachsene Leser hat vielfältige Deutungen gefunden: ist er das Dokument einer misanthropischen Neurose, der Inbegriff des welterobernden bürgerlichen homo oeconomicus, oder ein widerspenstiger Pilger in Gottes übergreifendem unentrinnbaren Plan? In seiner Komplexität ist er in neuer Lektüre auch für heutige Leser aktuell.
Bd. 39, 2017, 144 S., 29,90 €, br., ISBN 978-3-643-13836-1

Wolfgang Häde
Anschuldigungen und Antwort des Glaubens
Wahrnehmung von Christen in türkischen Tageszeitungen und Maßstäbe für eine christliche Reaktion
Die Türkei gilt als Brücke zwischen Europa und Asien und wurde lange Zeit als Beispiel für eine islamisch bestimmte, aber doch demokratische Gesellschaftsordnung zitiert. Das Verhältnis von Staat und Gesellschaft zu den christlichen Minderheiten im Land war jedoch nie frei von Spannungen. Die vorliegende Studie untersucht, wie türkische Tageszeitungen als Sprachrohre verschiedener soziopolitischer Milieus der Türkei Christen und ihren Glauben wahrnehmen. Religiöse, historische und politische Hintergründe der vorwiegend negativen Wahrnehmungen werden herausgearbeitet. Die missionswissenschaftliche Arbeit versucht abschließend, biblisch-theologisch begründete Reaktionen für Christen in der Türkei und in ähnlichen Kontexten nahezulegen.
Bd. 38, 2017, 310 S., 34,90 €, br., ISBN 978-3-643-13679-4

Christian Pohl
Evangelische Mission in Tanga und im Digoland
Der Beitrag einheimischer Mitarbeitender zur Kirchwerdung 1890 – 1925
Einheimische Mitarbeitende wirkten Ende des 19. Jahrhunderts von Anfang an beim Aufbau der Kirche in Tanga und dem angrenzenden Digoland mit (heutiges Tansania). Ihr inhaltlicher und organisatorischer Beitrag stieg im Lauf dieses Prozesses an. Während der durch den Ersten Weltkrieg bedingten Phase der Eigenständigkeit führten sie das kirchliche Leben selbständig weiter. Nach der Rückkehr der Missionare bis zur formellen Unabhängigkeit der Kirche war ihre Mitwirkung substantiell. Sie waren Akteure mit Handlungsmacht (agency), die durch die Aufnahme der Einflüsse deutscher Mitarbeitender und lokaler Komponenten eigene Akzente setzten und der Kirche ihr spezifisches Profil gaben, so dass eine hybride Form entstand.
Bd. 37, 2016, 310 S., 34,90 €, br., ISBN 978-3-643-13415-8

LIT Verlag Berlin – Münster – Wien – Zürich – London
Auslieferung Deutschland / Österreich / Schweiz: siehe Impressumsseite

Kambale Jean-Bosco Kahongya Bwiruka
Das Phänomen Hexenkinder in Goma
Religiöse Deutungen und Ansätze sozialer Arbeit christlicher Kirchen und Bewegungen
im Kontext der Krisenregion des Ost-Kongo
In den letzten Jahrzehnten haben Hexereianklagen gegen Kinder in verschiedenen Ländern Afrikas
deutlich zugenommen. So auch in der im Osten der Demokratischen Republik Kongo gelegenen Stadt
Goma. Die Situation des Ostkongo ist seit vielen Jahren durch Krieg und Gewalt bestimmt. Vor diesem Hintergrund beschreibt die Arbeit dämonologische Vorstellungen, die in der Bevölkerung weit
verbreitet sind, und analysiert die Art und Weise, wie verschiedene Kirchen und christliche Bewegungen mit dem Phänomen Hexenkinder umgehen. Der Verfasser plädiert für ein neues Verständnis
des prophetischen Auftrages der christlichen Kirchen angesichts der akuten Notlage, in der sich die
Menschen in dieser Region befinden, nicht zuletzt die Kinder unter ihnen.
Bd. 36, 2016, 336 S., 39,90 €, br., ISBN 978-3-643-13263-5

John O'Brien
Pakistan – The Instrumentalization of Islam
Political Manipulation of Islamic Theology in Pakistani History
This book studies Islam's place in Pakistani history and how it has been continually exploited by
successive regimes. Using Islam as a final political argument weakened it as a basis of national integration. Playing the Islamic card led to ever increasing Islamist demands. Jihadists violently vied to
uphold 'true Islam', often by targeting minorities. Such self-serving political manipulation is deconstructed in reflection on key theological debates in Islam.
vol. 35, 2015, 568 pp., 69,90 €, br., ISBN 978-3-643-90701-1

Elmar Spohn
Zwischen Anpassung, Affinität und Resistenz
Die Glaubens- und Gemeinschaftsmissionen in der Zeit des Nationalsozialismus
Diese Studie stellt erstmalig die Geschichte der Glaubens- und Gemeinschaftsmissionen bzw. der
evangelikalen Missionsgesellschaften in der NS-Zeit dar. An Äußerungen der Missionsblätter und
acht biographischen Einzelstudien wird aufgezeigt, wie man zum Nationalsozialismus stand. Dabei
kristallisierte sich ein Positionenspektrum heraus, welches von NS-Affinität bis Verfolgung reicht.
Darauffolgend wird der Umgang mit der Schuldfrage dokumentiert. Die abschließende kritische Analyse macht deutlich, dass sich die politische Ethik dieser Missionen meist nur in Obrigkeitsgehorsam
zeigte.
Bd. 34, 2016, 496 S., 54,90 €, br., ISBN 978-3-643-13213-0

Barbara Jordans
Zwischen Dienen in Demut und selbständiger Arbeit
Die ersten Missionsschwestern der Rheinischen Mission auf Sumatra 1890 – 1920
Missionsschwestern auf Sumatra wurden in der Forschung bisher kaum beachtet. Ihr Auftrag lautete,
in Demut zu dienen und sich um die einheimischen Frauen zu kümmern. Daneben begründeten sie
eine heute noch bestehende Schwesterngemeinschaft, bemühten sich um bessere Arbeitsbedingungen
und sicherten sich die Anerkennung ihrer Arbeit. Anhand ihrer Briefe und Berichte zeigt Barbara
Jordans, in wieweit sie dabei eigene Ideen und Vorstellungen umsetzen konnten, ohne die Grenzen
des zeitgenössischen Frauenbildes zu überschreiten.
Bd. 33, 2015, 186 S., 29,90 €, br., ISBN 978-3-643-13072-3

Claudia Währisch-Oblau; Henning Wrogemann (Eds.)
Witchcraft, Demons and Deliverance
A Global Conversation on an Intercultural Challenge
Beliefs in witchcraft and demons still shape many societies and seem to be increasing rather than disappearing with modernization and urbanization. Witch hunts in Africa and Asia show the scope of the
problem. The deliverance practices of Pentecostal and charismatic churches are widely controversial
and their effects rather ambiguous. The contributions in this volume, written by experts and practitioners from four continents, analyze these phenomena from the perspectives of intercultural theology,
anthropology and ethnology and describe the responses of Catholic and Protestant churches.
Bd. 32, 2015, 324 S., 34,90 €, br., ISBN 978-3-643-90657-1

LIT Verlag Berlin – Münster – Wien – Zürich – London

Auslieferung Deutschland / Österreich / Schweiz: siehe Impressumsseite

Uta Ihrke-Buchroth
Religious Mobility and Social Aspirations of Neopentecostals in Lima, Peru
This book investigates the religious and social background of members of neopentecostal mega-churches in Lima, Peru. It examines from a sociological perspective the social factors of religious mobility of neopentecostals to and between these churches. The findings address the question whether religious mobility of neopentecostals serves as a springboard for upward social mobility.
Bd. 31, 2014, 232 S., 34,90 €, br., ISBN 978-3-643-90556-7

Malte Rhinow
Eine kurze koreanische Kirchengeschichte bis 1910
Rechtzeitig zur Vollversammlung des ÖRK in Busan erscheint diese dem neuesten Stand der Forschung entsprechende Darstellung der frühen koreanischen Kirchengeschichte in deutscher Sprache. „Malte Rhinow hat eine beeindruckende Studie vorgelegt, die auf akribischem Quellenstudium basiert. Er erschließt ein umfangreiches Archivmaterial in koreanischer Sprache ... und erbringt durch die Auswertung schwer zugänglicher Texte eine pionierhafte Forschungsleistung. Die Untersuchung erlaubt einen vertieften Einblick in die Kirchengeschichte der verschiedenen christlichen Konfessionen Koreas". (aus dem Vorwort)
Bd. 29, 2013, 240 S., 24,90 €, br., ISBN 978-3-643-90247-4

Henning Wrogemann
Den Glanz widerspiegeln
Vom Sinn der christlichen Mission, ihren Kraftquellen und Ausdrucksgestalten. Interkulturelle Impulse für deutsche Kontexte
Das Thema Mission hat bei den deutschen Kirchen in den letzten Jahren wieder an Bedeutung gewonnen. Doch was genau ist der Sinn dieser Mission und welche Arbeitsfelder in Gemeinden, Kirchen und Gesellschaft sind als „missionarisch" zu bezeichnen? Was sind die Kraftquellen missionarischen Handelns? Wie steht es um die Erfahrbarkeit des Glaubens in Leiblichkeit und Heilung, in missionarischer Existenz und interreligiösem Dialog? Entwickelt wird ein doxologisches Missionsverständnis, in dem es um sichtbare Ausdrucksgestalten des christlichen Glaubens in heilsamen Kräften und Atmosphären geht.
Bd. 28, 2. Aufl. 2012, 288 S., 19,90 €, br., ISBN 978-3-643-11759-5

Gabriela Hofstetter
„Gehet hin und pfleget"
Basler Missionarinnen im Dienst der Ärztlichen Mission in Asien und Afrika (1892–1945)
Bd. 27, 2012, 248 S., 25,90 €, br., ISBN 978-3-643-80126-5

Edwin Udoye
Resolving the Prevailing Conflicts between Christianity and African (Igbo) Traditional Religion through Inculturation
Bd. 26, 2011, 416 S., 34,90 €, br., ISBN 978-3-643-90116-3

Apeliften Christian B. Sihombing
Mystik und Dialog der Religionen
Ein Vergleich mystischen Denkens im Protestantismus, im Sufismus und in der Kebatinan und seine Bedeutung für den interreligiösen Dialog in Indonesien
Bd. 25, 2012, 336 S., 29,90 €, br., ISBN 978-3-643-10976-7

Sylvester B. Kahakwa
A Haya-African Interpretation of the Christian Concept of God
A Study of an Invocation of the Deity in a Threefold Form for Indigenising and Understanding the Christian Trinitarian Model
vol. 24, 2010, 392 pp., 39,90 €, br., ISBN 978-3-643-10436-6

LIT Verlag Berlin – Münster – Wien – Zürich – London
Auslieferung Deutschland / Österreich / Schweiz: siehe Impressumsseite

Kirchen in der Weltgesellschaft
hrsg. von Prof. Dr. Dieter Becker (Neuendettelsau) und Prof. Dr. Andreas Nehring
(Erlangen-Nürnberg)

Liping Tu
Die chinesisch-christlichen Gemeinden in Deutschland
Ihre religionspädagogischen Aufgaben und Möglichkeiten
Die Herausforderungen für die Mitglieder chinesisch-christlicher Migrantengemeinden in Deutschland sind immens. Zugleich bieten sich ihnen enorme Möglichkeiten der Integration und der Persönlichkeitsentwicklung, wenn sie sich dem neuen soziokulturellen Umfeld öffnen und es aktiv zu entdecken beginnen. Die Autorin zeigt Spannungsfelder und Entwicklungspotentiale für die erste Generation von chinesischen Migranten auf. Zugleich eröffnet sie in einem kulturgeschichtlichen Abriss einen tieferen Einblick in die Geschichte und die aktuelle gesellschaftspolitische Situation in China.
Bd. 11, 2017, 250 S., 34,90 €, br., ISBN 978-3-643-13654-1

Karl-Fritz Daiber
Protestantismus und konfuzianische Kultur
Aspekte ihrer Zuordnung in China und Südkorea
Dass es einen vitalen chinesischen und koreanischen Protestantismus gibt, wird von Fremden, die Korea oder China besuchen, vielfach übersehen. Dass China und Korea immer noch vom konfuzianischen Erbe mitgeprägt sind, wird von manchen inländischen Analytikern nicht selten ignoriert. Dem entgegen geht es dem Verfasser darum, Spuren des Ineinanders von Protestantismus und konfuzianischer Kultur zu entdecken. Die deutsche Diskussion der Chinamission um 1700 und die Taiping-Revolution finden besonderes Interesse.
Bd. 10, 2017, 160 S., 29,90 €, br., ISBN 978-3-643-13653-4

Harald Stuntebeck
Canudos
Eine sozial-religiöse Volksbewegung in Brasilien und ihre pastorale Wirkungsgeschichte
Angeregt durch den Roman „Der Krieg am Ende der Welt" von Mario Vargas Llosa, führt die Suche nach den historischen Hintergründen in den Sertão, eine Region im Nordosten Brasiliens: Schauplatz einer religiösen Sozialbewegung, die nach dem Ort „Canudos" benannt wird. Sie gewann in der zweiten Hälfte des 19. Jahrhunderts an Bedeutung, weil sie Landlose und andere Bedrängte anzog, aber kirchlich beargwöhnt und militärisch bekämpft wurde. Die dramatische Geschichte und ihre memoriale sowie pastorale Rezeption bis in die Gegenwart sind Gegenstand des vorliegenden Buches. Harald Stuntebeck legt nach intensiver Quellenrecherche eine umfassende deutschsprachige Darstellung über Canudos vor – mit besonderem Gespür für theologisch-pastorale Dimensionen und zugleich wachem Blick auf die soziale und religiöse Situation der Gegenwart in Brasilien.
Bd. 9, 2016, 672 S., 69,90 €, br., ISBN 978-3-643-13021-1

Daniel Frei
Die Pädagogik der Bekehrung
Sozialisation in chilenischen Pfingstkirchen
Bd. 8, 2011, 456 S., 31,90 €, br., ISBN 978-3-643-80083-1

Jozef Hehanussa
Der Molukkenkonflikt von 1999
Zur Rolle der Protestantischen Kirche (GPM) in der Gesellschaft
Bd. 7, 2013, 448 S., 49,90 €, br., ISBN 978-3-643-10906-4

Marceli Fritz-Winkel
Zur Zukunft der Evangelischen Kirche Lutherischen Bekenntnisses in Brasilien
Aspekte ihrer Attraktivität im Vergleich mit der Umbanda und der neopentekostalen Igreja Universal do Reino de Deus
Bd. 6, 2012, 248 S., 24,90 €, br., ISBN 978-3-643-10888-3

LIT Verlag Berlin – Münster – Wien – Zürich – London
Auslieferung Deutschland / Österreich / Schweiz: siehe Impressumsseite